What do You Think?

Conversations about Faith and Spirituality in the New Millennium

BY STEPHEN FOWLER

Foreword

This work is a collection of articles covering
numerous sub-topics to faith and spirituality.
Everyone who provided editorial advice commented
that the work is thought provoking.

The author has included various references to
both popular culture as well as some more obscure
but still relevant contributions to the public stores of
creativity. He also shares a few personal
experiences for the reader's consideration.

The tone of the articles themselves often
comes off as editorial. It is plainspoken and
succinct. There is a great deal of commentary that
can be applied to daily life. Although the general
subjects are faith and spirituality, the reader will find
little if any content that can be thought of as ethereal
or astral.

The author is looking to generate
conversation. No final answers to spiritual or faith
related questions can be found in this text. What the
reader will find is a framework to ask the questions
that will help them to define their own spirituality or

lack thereof. Whether you worship formally or not whether you are a believer or not, whether you are reformist or fundamentalist, and no matter your walk of life, you will find plenty in this work to challenge your preconceptions about faith, spirituality, and religion.

This work can be read cover to cover, or the reader can choose to read whichever articles interests him or her the most, first, and if their interest is piqued, they may continue on, reading other articles as well.

It is recommended, although not necessary, that the reader take time to reflect on each individual article before proceeding to the next. It may very well be that a greater, more meaningful journey through life awaits the reader upon concluding their internalization of this work.

Author's Note

As I have come to the end of this project, I have come to realize that by releasing it publicly, I am essentially putting myself on notice as to how I ought to live the rest of my life. If this work becomes widely circulated, for good or ill, there will be more people observing me and my life choices. While it is my hope that those choices will be pleasing to both readers and non-readers of this work alike, there are certain to be those who will look for reasons to criticize me. I don't control that. I can only hope to be able to look myself in the mirror before I turn in each night and believe that my actions for that day were in line with what God would wish from me.

The reader will come to a point in the text in which I come across as being unapologetic for whatever material success this work may have. I am not about to change that stance herein. I do however, wish to assure the reader that I will look upon myself not as being entitled to do whatever I please for my own personal needs with the revenue from this project, but rather (to a large extent) as the steward of that revenue. While I anticipate using some of the revenue to make myself whole with my creditors and to get back to the point where I have a home and an automobile that are in good repair, as well as to spend some money on a much needed and perhaps well-earned vacation from time to time.

That said, I also intend to give back. If possible, I will give back to Second Congregational Church, and Enfield Loaves and Fishes, both of which were there to help me in times of great need. I also anticipate donating to research for the cure of ovarian cancer, the ASPCA, and WNPR among others. For the purpose of maintaining a modicum of privacy, I will add here that the surest way for any supposed charitable to get themselves off of my list of who I will give back to, is to call me at my home.

For Openers

I don't remember my baptism. I do recall a conversation that I had with my parents, particularly my mother, when I was five or six years old. I was beginning to ask questions about religion. My parents must have been conversing and the words *Christian* and *Jewish* came up. I must have wanted to know which I was, but I specifically recall prefacing my question with "Mom, we're Jewish, right?" She said, "No, Stephen, we're Christian.

Now because of my upbringing, my experiences, and the fact that I can still recite the Apostles Creed without cringing or flinching, I do consider myself today to be a follower of the Christian faith. However, I think it's safe to assume that you, my reader, will not conclude upon reading this, that it is an exclusively Christian text. To be sure, there may very well be some who will conclude on their own judgment that I am not Christian. While I will not accept their judgment, I would defend to the death their right to make it.

The purpose of this text is to share the thinking of a congregant of a parish of The United Church of Christ with people and clergy of many faiths as well as those who consider themselves to be without faith, in an attempt to generate thought and discussion. I do not pretend to be a profession[al] theologian in any capacity. What I am is a living, breathing, thinking human being, who is attempting to use the brain given to him by a Creative Force which I will call God, and to whom I will assign th[e] masculine pronouns in this writing, in an attempt t[o] come to terms with my understanding of that force to the best of my ability.

I anticipate that this text will ask a great man[y] more questions than it answers. Still in all, it shou[ld] become apparent to the reader that I have given extensive thought to the matters of faith, religion, and spirituality. If I can get you to do the same, I will accept that as a success.

As part of the editing process, the phrase "What do you think?" was added to the title of this work. You may find it curious that I am asking what you think, and then proceeding with extensively telling you what *I* think. That is why I have left open pages aside each article, into which encourage you to write down what *you* think. I suggest using "sticky notes" in case you are lendin[g] this work to someone else or borrowing it from the library. I am hopeful of setting up a blog as part o[f] website to go along with this work. I will look to

ld submissions which are appropriate and that
nallenge my thinking as well as that of others.

You are reading what is essentially the second
lition of this work, which includes several
dditional articles that did not appear in the first
lition. Because the first edition was released prior
the 2016 national election, there was no reference
the person who succeeded President Barack
bama to residency in the White House. As it is my
ish to minimize discussion of politics in this work,
e reader will notice that I have made no attempt to
odate the text in any way to recognize change with
spect to the individual who presently resides in the
hite House.

May God bless you, and may He forgive me
y place in this text in which I may step out of line.

Contents

What Father Hybel Emphasized

I anticipate covering all sorts of different ground as I proceed with this effort, and as I sit at my keyboard for the first time, I can't be certain as to which topic will come after which. I anticipate jumping all around, but I will start chronologically, with the earliest influences on my personal faith. I can't do that without referring to the Reverend Robert Hybel, who served as the spiritual leader at St. Luke's Episcopal Church in Somers, New York from the 1950s into the 1980s. I attended that church fairly regularly as a small child, being taken there on Sunday mornings by my parents and sometimes my grandmother.

The service was exceedingly liturgical but mercifully brief, as Father Hybel had to perform a subsequent service at St. James Church in North Salem, New York, and had to build in time to travel from one parish to the other. While school was in session it was customary for Father Hybel to deliver a short "children's sermon" of sorts, right after the Gospel lesson and just before we were sent off to

Sunday school. The balance of the service would be attended only by the adults.

To be sure, my primary motivation for attending church in those days was the close proximity of the Luncheonette, which allowed me to purchase baseball cards or football cards after service with the ten cents allowance that I had earned doing my chores over the previous week. When I grew into my "tweens" as we call them now, I elected to stay for the balance of the service, forgoing the Sunday school program. Eventually I decided that church wasn't for me and stopped attending altogether. In hindsight, I would characterize this as a suspension of my attendance, but that is a subject for later in this text. For now, I need to share that again in hindsight, the influence that Father Hybel had on my in my formative years appears to have been incalculable. Older folks, who have studied life and perhaps faith, tend to understand that the impact of adults on the young is profound, and in some instances tragically and irreversibly traumatic. Happily, I can report that to the best of my knowledge, Father Hybel positively influenced everyone whose paths he crossed.

Most significantly, I wish to share the two snippets of the New Testament scripture to which Father Hybel referred most frequently. If anyone from his family reads this, I'm sure they will agree. I will reference the gospel according to Matthew, with which am most familiar although these quotes may appear in other gospels as well, I am referring to two quotes in particular. First, "Judge not, lest ye thyself be judged" and second, "He who exalts himself shall be humbled, and he who humbles himself shall be exalted". I heard Father Hybel repeat these two phrases more times than I can count. I know that I have judged many people, and that I have exalted myself. But I like to believe that I can catch myself doing these things now.

Could Jesus have died of kidney failure?

Here's where I start jumping around.

In April, 2001, Charlie Ward who was a player for the NBA's New York Knicks after starring in both football and basketball at Florida State University and winning the Heisman Trophy, created a stir in the media by blaming the Jews for persecuting Jesus. New York media in particular could not resist the temptation to raise this discussion to absurd heights based on the relatively high profile of the individual making the accusations. I found the flap to be altogether amusing, although it did not occur to me at the time that I might be writing about it later.

In any church that I have ever attended, if the subject came up, it was generally agreed that we *all* killed Jesus. Loosely, I would take that to include everyone who may have had the opportunity to prevent his crucifixion from taking place, but let it happen anyway. That could include Roman soldiers, Jews, and any manner of polytheists or non-believers who may have lived in or near Jerusalem at the time.

But the main takeaway that I had from the whole Charlie Ward dust up was my realization that we would not be talking about Jesus today if he had died from kidney failure or heart disease. Scripture tells us of how Jesus knew how he was going to die and when. He made numerous attempts to share this knowledge with his followers, but we get the sense that they were not able to grasp what he was saying.

So yes, "the Jews" did persecute Jesus. And so did everyone else. And if you are a Christian, I imagine you would believe that Jesus forgave them all. According to scripture, as he hung on the cross, Jesus said, "Forgive them Father; they know not what they do". So, I guess that if God acceded to his son's wishes, he had to have forgiven the Jews, the Troglodytes, the Druids, the followers of Zeus and Apollo, the Wiccans, the Muslims etc. He probably even would have bitten down real hard and forgiven Charlie Ward as well.

Does God really want us to praise Him all the time?

A lot of this text is about what people believe. I anticipate writing on the notions of monotheism, polytheism and atheism later. But if we assume the existence of God, I must ask, ought we not to spend some time trying to grapple with the nature of this deity? Would it not be safe to accept the notion that this God is altogether wiser and more sophisticated than we are? I don't see God as being someone who needs His ego boosted all that much.

If there is a God, and God is omnipotent, then He knows if your worship and praise is genuine. So for example, if you are waving your arms around over your heads during worship service, one may wonder who you are looking to impress. If it is God, then you needn't bother, since God knows if you are sincere or not. If you are trying to impress people who see you praising God, you should consider that you may be coming off as insincere.

It has been brought to my attention that in some churches, the congregation is expressing genuine enthusiasm when they are waving their arms in the air. I confess that I come from a stuffy New England Protestant background, but I also know that my experience at the end of the Alpha program with a large contingent from The Church of the Living God was not a sensation of exuberance, but rather one of almost feeling coerced. People know in their hearts if they are being genuine or phony, and if their enthusiasm is indeed genuine, then it is not for me to judge them. I would just add that Evangelical Christians in particular, need to be cautious about turning people off.

At one church that I attended, I remember meeting a guy who looked forward to going to heaven, which sounds like a good thing to look forward to, assuming one believes in it. What I found curious was his reason for it. He said he was looking forward to being able to spend all of his time praising God and Praising Jesus. Sounds like fun, doesn't it? I hope he wasn't saying this for my benefit. It just seems to me that a God who created everything would be more interested in having sentient beings attempt to do His will to the best of their understanding, than having them praise him twenty-four hours a day. I somehow think that the person who conveyed this notion of what to do in heaven to me genuinely wants to do good in the world. I have seen him do good works in less than optimal circumstances with no thought of personal material gain. I can easily envision "Bible Thumpers" sharing the same notion of what to do in heaven, as they sanctimoniously pontificate to all of us plebes. But that wasn't the case with this guy. He's a good guy. I just hope he gets to read this, and maybe re-imagines what to do in heaven when he might get there.

I will throw out this possibility. . .   In heaven, every week is three days long. There's Saturday, Sunday, and either a holiday Monday or Friday depending on your preference. So yes, you are in temple, mosque, church, or whatever other choice you make for your place of worship for a portion of every third day. There, you pray for the souls of those who still dwell on the planet from which you came. You pray for peace, you pray for those who are suffering there, you praise God and your chosen prophet. But you still have the rest of that day and the other two days to chill, hang out with family and friends, recreate as you see fit, and maybe take on an odd errand or two for God if you are up to it. No one will stop you from praying or praising while you are not at formal worship if that is really what you want to do. It just isn't required.

Jesus never wrote anything down

Father Hybel was explicit in his emphasis of this point. And while his sermons necessarily squared with something from the assigned scripture for the particular service depending on the week of the church year, you could count on being reminded of this point several times a year if you attended St. Luke's Church.

The take-away from this could be extended to the Old Testament of the Bible, but to keep to the immediate point, anything you read in the New Testament which is attributed to Jesus is a quote, reported by a scribe several decades after the fact. There are a few historical cross references outside of biblical scripture attesting to Jesus of Nazareth, and this is helpful to historians be they of the Christian faith, another faith, agnostic or even atheist. We know that he lived, when he lived and where he lived. We have to speculate as to what he said. Our best information about what he may have said apparently comes from the gospels of Mark, Matthew, Luke and John, as they appear in the New Testament.

The gospels are the one place in sacred scripture where we have multiple accounts of the same events. Interestingly, Father Hybel shared the notion of four witnesses to a car accident. They could all have been standing at four different corners of a four-way intersection, and when the police obtained their accounts, they got four different versions, each varying in some way or ways from the other three. As such, you are left with questions with unclear answers such as, "How many angels appeared at the entrance of the tomb on Easter Morning?" The answer may be considered moot and unimportant, but it is interesting that there is a question. What is more important is that we do have multiple testimonies to a single set of events. In no other place in the Bible, other than in the New Testament, does this occur.

Still, the question occurs, "Why didn't Jesus write anything down?" We know he was well educated, and that he had the intellectual capacity to write. For all we know, he may have written some things down prior to his ministry, perhaps during his carpentry apprenticeship. Being an apprentice, he may have had to take down a lunch order such as 2 Kung Pau Chicken, 1 Pepper Steak and 1 Pork Lo Mein. Such writing however, would have been impertinent to his ministry, and would not have survived two thousand years of weathering. So, we are back to the notion that Jesus never wrote anything down. And we are also back to speculating as to why he did not.

Father Hybel had a hypothesis, which I will paraphrase here. It would have run in direct contradiction to his job description, i.e. he wasn't supposed to write anything down. God might have surmised in this manner . . . "Look son, they are going to mess this up anyway. You can't give them any excuses to blame it on you. We are forgiving them for their sins and hopefully all moving on, but many of them are already trying to pass off the Old Testament as being written by me. If you write anything down, it can be characterized as being written by me. Some of them will figure things out on their own, such as what I would wish for them to do. If they get that we are merciful and that we want them to treat each other well, they can hopefully pass that message down through history. Does it come from us? Yes. Should we write any of it down? Perhaps it's not such a good idea."

Why did Jesus show up 2000 years ago instead of now, or some other time?

Here's where I like to cite the movie "Oh God" from the late 1970s. People past their 40's probably remember this one. It starred George Burns, John Denver, and Terri Garr. You can still order a copy of this movie from your local library.

In the movie, God (George Burns) speaks to Jerry Landers (John Denver) who is working as a grocery clerk. Of course, He only does it when Jerry is alone, and in any event, no one else can see him or hear him. Jerry obediently tries to share God's message with everyone around him and ultimately gets interviewed by the local T.V. station. He is subject to all manner of ridicule and humiliation, as he can never prove that God spoke to him. Even his wife questions his sanity.

He shares the misery he is dealing with, with God. At one point, he is challenged to have God appear in court. He shows God the list of questions that have been prepared for Him to answer. Remarkably, God agrees to appear. The time for him to appear comes and at first it appears that God is blowing Jerry off, causing him even further embarrassment. However, God finally does show up, stunning everyone in the courtroom with his appearance. He appears as a retired elderly cigar smoking fisherman. While he answers the questions, the court stenographer dutifully types his answers down. There is even a cassette tape recording being made of the event.

When God decides that he has answered enough questions, he stands up and walks out of the courthouse. During his walk out, he becomes invisible, but you can still hear his footfalls, and finally, the main entrance door to the courthouse opens and then closes, apparently all by itself. Everyone in attendance is astonished.

After the fact, all of the lawyer's questions can be heard on the cassette tape and seen on the stenographic record. However, all of God's responses have disappeared, and no record of them, written or otherwise, remains. Everyone who was witness to the event is left to decide for themselves. Did this happen, or not? The same goes for Jesus' ministry. It happened before DVDs, I Pads, E-Pads and / or any other such devices had been invented. It happened before the invention of the printing press. It happened before many of the world's modern languages came into being. To be sure, it can safely be assumed that if a re-make of "Oh,

God" were done now, all of God's appearances would once again mysteriously vanish from record, no matter what manner of current technological devices were used to record it.

Think about it. Assuming for the moment (with apologies to all of the atheist readers) that there is a creative force in the universe that we call God or something else, it should be safe to say that the creative force is not only more powerful than us, it is also vastly more sophisticated than we are. Would it (He) not know what humans would become capable of doing? Most of us observe life in the modern day and conclude that there is not a lot in the way of overt divine intervention taking place. If you buy into Christianity, you do accept that there was intervention just over 2,000 years ago. But you must accept it without proof.

So here we are once again, being left to speculate. How about this for speculation? It happened when it happened, on purpose. It happened at a time that agreed with God's plan and given His understanding of our technological advancement to that point. It happened when it happened because we are supposed to have faith. We are supposed to be faithful. We are *not supposed* to rely on empirical "proof".

Religious conversion at gunpoint?

I can sense that some of the non-Christian readers may be starting to get squeamish, so it's probably time to shift to a more ecumenical topic now. For this topic, I will cite Malala Yousafzai's book, <u>I am Malala.</u> I think this is appropriate in response to some think tanks recent contributions to public discussion, that of trashing Islam in all of its iterations.

For those not familiar, Malala is a young woman who grew up in Pakistan in a town bordering Afghanistan. Her father founded and ran schools that educated girls along with boys. Malala attended those schools. At that time, the Taliban was able to establish a territorial foothold in the area where she lived. They attempted to implement Sharia law and were successful for a time in some areas. They threatened schools such has hers. One day, they stopped the bus on which she and her classmates were being transported. They shot at her and hit her in the face with their bullets. She survived, but she had to be treated in England. Eventually, she and her family established residence there. Ultimately, she traveled to New York and addressed the United Nations at the age of sixteen regarding the importance of education for girls and women in the world. She became the youngest person to ever win the Nobel Peace Prize.

Malala is Islamic. From reading her book, one can easily surmise that she does not subscribe to an extremist interpretation of Sharia law. She does not espouse violence, or the suppression of women in any manner. How can this be? I will leave that to our reactionary geniuses to figure out. In any event, she is representative of the religion that gets most singled out for extremism today.

To be sure, it might be helpful if more of the Islamic leadership would become more vocal in its opposition to the atrocities perpetrated by the extremists. Some cultural icons such as NBA Hall of Famer Kareem Abdul Jabbar who has leveraged his fame in contributing columns to Time magazine periodically, Yusuf Islam (a.k.a. Cat Stevens) and most recently Muhammed Ali have strongly condemned the violent acts of so-called Islamic extremists. We need more Muslims like them to speak out. The rest of us need to respect and appreciate those Muslims who are speaking out, as there's are acts of bravery in light of the fact that they are making targets of themselves in the eyes of the extremists.

The overwhelming majority of proclaimed Muslims whether they are Shiite or Sunni, disavow themselves from the extremists. It would be analogous to some extent to if a very small faction of self-proclaimed Christians were to (let's just say) blow up women's health clinics and characterize anyone who objected to their tactics as being anti-Christian.

But we do know that these self-avowed Islamic extremists are going around killing and threatening to kill all *infidels*, unless they will convert to their brand of Islam. If I could speak with them, I would wish to ask (albeit rhetorically), "Do you really think you can get someone to genuinely convert to your (oh, so sorry), I mean, *the* true religion by pointing a gun to their head?"

Here's the thing. Many religious adults had some sort of religious upbringing through their family. If you are one of them, your parents either took you with them to temple, church, mosque, or wherever else they went when you were a child. That was your first exposure to God, Yahweh, Jehovah, Allah or whatever name you prefer. But at some point, you must decide for yourself what you believe. Once you have done that, it is a good idea to face challenges to your beliefs and faith as they come along during your life, but that is a subject for later. For now, the emphasis is that each person's faith or lack thereof is deeply personal.

Violent extremists, besides being thin-skinned, must be truly ignorant if they think that they can scare someone into genuinely converting to *the one and only true faith* by putting a gun to their head. You can probably get someone to assure you that they have converted to your religion with your scare tactics, but all you will have secured would be temporary lip-service given under duress. As soon as you leave them and remove your gun from their face in order to point it at someone else's, their true beliefs that have been built up over a lifetime will

kick right back in. So, it appears that religious conversion at gunpoint does not work. Never did, never will.

The 6th Grader who wanted to know about atheism

In my capacity as a substitute teacher in one instance, I had to cover ground with respect to the evolution (if you will) of religion, with a 6th grade class. We discussed the polytheism of the ancient Greeks, Romans and Egyptians. Then we moved on to the notion of monotheism, which was first conceptualized by the Jews. In this way, the students were able to understand the historical progression of religion in the world, and perhaps gain some sense of how it evolved in terms of sophistication. The lesson plan did not call for fast forwarding through Galileo's scientific discoveries and how they put him at odds with the hierarchy of the Roman Catholic Church, but I did get the opportunity to field a question from one student who wanted to know about atheism.

Some within the field of education may be curious as to how I handled the situation, keeping in mind that there were three paraprofessionals in attendance at the time. My brief preamble included a compulsory glance at the clock and the remark that I thought we could spend a few moments on the subject. This leads back to my discussion about religious conversion at gunpoint to some extent, but the way I put it back to the student and her classmates was by citing the renowned quantum physicist Stephen Hawking. A fair number of the students had heard of him, which was helpful. My point to them was that Mr. Hawking is an avowed atheist, but that despite his extensive and profound contributions to science, particularly astrophysics and quantum mechanics, he has not been able to convince many among the world's human population including many renowned scientists of the non-existence of God. He has not been able to prove God's non-existence either via science or any other manner of logical thinking to the satisfaction of the world's faithful.

I need to share here that a review of the concluding chapter of Mr. Hawking's book "A Short History of Time" does not fully support the assertion that he is an atheist. Certainly, he is not a devout Christian, but it would be fairer to cast him as an agnostic than as an atheist. Still, much of his scientific discussion has been employed by atheists in their denial of the existence of God.

Atheism is itself a belief system. It is simply the belief that God does not exist. It may be frustrating to some atheists to realize that they cannot convince the faithful among us that God does not exist, just as the converse is true in that the faithful cannot scientifically prove God's existence to the satisfaction of the atheists.

In any event, I concluded my discussion with the statement that no one can be convinced of any religious conviction at gunpoint. I did not have time and it would not have been my place to determine who in the class considered themselves to be of which faith or without faith, but it was interesting that no one challenged any of my assertions. Also, I did not hear back from any of the paraprofessionals or any irate parents with respect to my discussion. Without the time that I would have needed and given that I was covering for another teacher in my capacity as a substitute, I regret that we were not able to delve into the topic to any greater depth. However, I do think that this subject and others like it would be excellent for generating discussion and deep thought in the classroom, which brings me to my next topic . . .

What place if any, does discussion of religion and faith have in the classroom?

I bet a lot more educators struggle with this question than care to admit it. We certainly spend time talking about how people should treat each other in the classroom. We talk about having respect for your classmates' right to learn. We discourage bullying. We try to get the students engaged in this discussion.

For many people of faith, the root of our understanding of how we should treat each other comes from our faith in a higher power. But we are scared to talk about it in the classroom for fear of rousing the ire of parents. I would not suggest that public school is any place for trying to convert impressionable young people to one formal religion or another. If I was a Muslim parent (let's just say) and I knew that my child's teacher was trying to convert them to another religion using my tax dollars, I don't think I would respond in a positive way

That being said, I do think we can have some discussion of faith in a public school setting without crossing the line. For instance, if I was teaching science and a student were to ask me about Intelligent Design, I would of course first preface my response with an obligatory glance at the clock and saying, "I think we have enough time to spend a few minutes discussing it".

My discussion would then go something like this . . . "First, we must understand that Intelligent Design is not science, it is theology. Science asks the question, "How?" Theology asks the question "Why?" Any time you hear a scientist discussing science and they use the word "why", they are moving into the realm of theology whether they want to admit it or not". Then I would simply state that Intelligent Design theorizes that everything natural was created by a higher power and leave it at that. I would suggest independent study for any student for whom this discussion may pique additional interest, and even suggest that they consider attending a church, temple, mosque or other place of worship, at least on an experimental basis.

Before moving on, I would suggest the viewing of an I-Max documentary simply named "Galapagos" that I once saw, which took a deep dive (pardon the pun) into the ecosystem of the Galapagos Islands archipelago off the coast of Ecuador. It was a masterful piece of cinematography, which concisely and simply discussed all the interactions and interrelationships between the vast number of land and aquatic animal and plant species that exist there. The balance of predator and prey, as well as symbiosis and all other manner of relationships are vividly depicted. At no time in the film is the notion of a higher power ever discussed. However, as the film progresses, the intricate and delicate balance of nature becomes increasingly apparent. The suggestion of creative genius becomes strikingly manifest.

For anyone who may not have considered the possibility of a creative force in the universe before seeing this film, I wonder what they would think after seeing it. If the thought hasn't at least occurred to them by the end of the film, they may want to consider checking themselves for a discernable pulse. I highly recommend showing this film which is altogether appropriate for any middle school or high school science class. The students will find it fascinating.

E = MC Squared. The soul lives on

Although I have preliminary certification to teach middle school in Massachusetts, I confess at the time of this writing that I am not comfortable to teach science. It was not my strong subject in grade school, and with the exception of one course that I had to take to satisfy the core curriculum requirement, I steered clear of it in college. I don't understand the science behind Einstein's theory of relativity to the point where I would presume to explain it to anyone else. But I do understand that he proved that energy can be transformed, but it can never be destroyed.

So, when we extend this conversation to the realm of theology, the question that naturally bubbles up is, "Whither the soul?" Is there not an energy that dwells within our mortal bodies, which builds up our lifetime memories, storing them in our brains? Does that energy not program its behavior patterns and makes adjustments as life's events transpire?

The question of how that energy is installed is subject for a later topic, but for now the question of what happens to that energy when the mortal body ceases to function suffices. The body after all, is not the source of the energy; it is simply the vessel in which the energy goes about its chosen tasks. Then when the body stops functioning, since the energy is not destroyed, we must logically conclude that it is released and transformed.

Beyond this we can only speculate, which I will happily do at various points throughout this text. But even our scientific and atheistic friends must accept that the energy that once resided in a mortal body still exists, unless they want to argue science with Albert Einstein. I for one don't have a prayer of winning that argument.

Does God have a sense of humor?

This article is about a dream that I had about my mother, Barbara. She passed on much sooner in life than most of her friends and family would have anticipated at the age of 73. She was stricken just under two years earlier with ovarian cancer, which had reached Stage IV by the time it was diagnosed.

Without going into a full biographical sketch, I will just say that beginning with what was in many respects a sheltered childhood and into a sheltered adult life into my late thirties, I remained for the most part, uncritical of my mother. It was not until after she had passed on that people made me more aware of what would be considered some of her foibles and shortcomings.

She had always been a spirited woman, full of life, love and charm. It could be said that among her loves were material possessions, although she would never have admitted this to anyone much less to herself. With that backdrop, I will share the following dream that I had to the best of my recollection.

I had this dream sometime after my mother's passing. She was in this dream, and I had an understanding that I was seeing her in a context beyond her earthly life. I was visiting her. She was in a kitchen in a house, which she understood to be hers, and she was cooking a meal. She had invited me for dinner. She was early on in her meal preparations and suggested that I take a tour of the rest of the house.

I decided to take her up on it, and walked toward the back and through the door exiting the kitchen. Beyond the door was a hall. There were rooms to either side. Many of the doors to the rooms were open and I could see into the rooms. Bedrooms were spacious, airy with bright sunlight shining in and were well appointed. There were other rooms as well that might have been dens, day rooms, living rooms and so on. There was a bank of stairs in the middle of the hall that you could take up to a loft level. At the top of the stairs was another hall with rooms to either side, followed by another set of doors, beyond which, the hall extended on even further.

Once again, there were rooms as well as halls to either side. I continued with my investigation of the house, but the halls and rooms just stretched on and on, with more banks of steps leading both up and down. A right turn or a left turn off the main hall just revealed more rooms, steps, and halls. At some point, it occurred to me that this might not be my mother's house; it might be God's house, thinking of the gospel scripture in which Jesus tells us, "In my father's house, there are many rooms." It was at this point that I heard or perhaps felt a voice. This will sound cliché, but it was a deep voice and a male voice with authority in it. The voice was not necessarily speaking to me, but seemingly more to itself or to anyone within earshot. The first thing I heard was gentle laughter. Then the voice said, "Yeah . . . she thinks it's her house!"

The cloned dog

I recall at one time attending a service in Delaware when I was visiting my mother and her friend John. This was after my stepfather had been diagnosed with Alzheimer's disease. My mother had moved their residence from New York to Delaware so they could better afford the nursing home costs.

The pastor, who was an elderly gentleman, gave a sermon in which he was addressing the phenomenon of cloning. He was trying to square theology with science as best he could, but he seemed to be having a pretty tough time of it. After the service, I found myself wrestling with the theological implications of cloning and not being able to come up with any solution that was comforting to me.

I recalled this service years later, when I heard the story of an obscenely wealthy couple who had a dog that they loved dearly. As the dog aged and its health began to fail, they decided to have the dog cloned before it died. A sample of the dog's DNA was harvested and after it passed away, a private consortium of scientists proceeded with cloning, having charged the couple a considerable fee up front and having obtained their signatures to all of the legal disclaimers and so forth.

From a physiological standpoint, the cloning was a success. The couple had their new old dog back as a puppy. But here's the rub. The personality of the cloned dog was not the same. The original dog had been a playful active dog, which often exhibited dominant behavior in social situations with other dogs. This new old dog was still affectionate, but much more subdued and submissive. The scientists had succeeded with the genetic copying of the dog, but it could be argued that they had not succeeded in installing the identical spirit. Clearly the cloned animal had a spirit, but it was not the same one. Apparently, the spirit of the new old dog had come from somewhere else, and not the science lab. Hmmmmm.

I imagine that this information might have been useful to the old pastor in Delaware, if he had it in time for his sermon on cloning.

If Jesus was "just a teacher", why does Christianity even exist?

I have one family member who I love dearly, who claims that Jesus was a "gentle teacher." Few would argue that, but there is the implication that that's all he was. That wouldn't explain to my satisfaction however, why we are still talking about him after 2000 years.

According to the Gospels in the New Testament, there was a great deal of tumult at the time of Jesus' crucifixion. The masses, who celebrated his triumphant entrance into Jerusalem on what came to be known as Palm Sunday, were bitterly disappointed by his failure to call everyone to arms to overthrow the hated Romans by the middle of the week. Then of course we have the last supper, his betrayal by Judas, the trials and the crucifixion itself. As the events transpired, his chosen followers came to fear for their lives, to the point where they all essentially hid in what could best be described as a small cottage, from Jews and Romans alike. This is a critical point. They feared for their lives!

Now, if that is the end of it, and Jesus was just a "gentle teacher", then would his followers have not just scurried into the night like so many cockroaches at their earliest opportunities and disappeared from Jerusalem to it outskirts and beyond, never to be heard from again? But that's not what happened.

The followers were transformed from fearing for their lives to being willing to accept imprisonment and / or martyrdom if it would come to that, all for the sake of "spreading the good news". They went from the depths of cowardice which had allowed them to deny him altogether, to the pinnacle of courage. That could not have happened just on account of following a "gentle teacher" who went around telling everyone that they needed to be nice to each other. It could perhaps have happened if he rose from the dead in some way, shape, or form, appeared to them and asked them to spread the word.

With Christianity as with any faith, there is the element of belief or lack thereof with which each must come to their own terms. The notion of resurrection is not something that one can wrap their head around like they can with a mathematical equation. How Jesus may have appeared to his followers is a subject that has been debated among self-proclaimed Christians. Even in the present day, it causes members and leaders of various churches to fall out from each other, calling each other despicable names and so forth. It is a curiosity to be sure.

The attitudes of Jesus' followers were profoundly transformed, and this happened after his death. This is as close to fact as one can get within the realm of theology. If we accept that this is due to his appearing to them, here is one response to the question of how it came about. To borrow a phrase from Hillary Clinton, "What difference does it make now?"

Strengthening one's faith

Faith can be placed in different things such as religion, people, or even sports teams. Faith can be challenged. We can become disillusioned with our faith. Events can cause us to question our faith. At this point, I just want to focus on intellectual challenges, I would just add that strong faith is faith that has accepted challenges and survived them. Faith can be thought of as a voluntary muscle. If you work to strengthen it, there is a better chance that it will survive future challenges. If you just let it lie dormant, it may weaken, and fail you when you most need it.

Faith can also work in tandem with intellectual discipline such as critical thinking skills. Here's an example.

There is a website, which everyone can check out for free, called religioustolerance.org. The site was put together by people in Toronto, ON, Canada. There are numerous interesting writings on the site, but one which particularly caught my attention had to do with the semi-god from Egyptian mythology named Horus. The site digs into the notion shared by some researchers that according to legend, Horus, whose name first appears in text from thousands of years before Jesus' birth, was crucified, buried, and raised from the dead three days later. The inference that can be made is that the information shared in the New Testament pertaining to Jesus' resurrection was copied from Egyptian mythology. This is discussed in detail in a book called <u>The Pagan Christ</u> by Thomas Harpur. If true, this assertion would debunk Christianity at its foundation.

Mr. Harpur sites three other historians or Egyptologists in the book, and anyone can do a deep dive into the controversy that stirred upon release of the book, but suffice it to say that the scholarship of Mr. Harpur as well as his three sources has (not surprisingly) been taken to task by numerous critics. As a layperson, I have neither the time nor the inclination to dig through all of the research on either side of the debate. I tend however, to fall back on the question of how Christianity could ever have survived beyond the first few days subsequent to Jesus' passing had it not been for the profound change in the attitude of his followers as discussed previously.

The main point here is just the rigor that one must accept in internalizing a challenge such as this one. If one simply accepts the assertion at face value, that is akin to weak faith that cannot or will not stand up to any challenge. On the other hand, it is not enough to simply reject such an assertion out of hand without thinking through the debate at some level and doing the necessary soul-searching. Ought we to use the brains we were given at birth? Would failure to do so not also be to fail as human beings?

People who were raised in the Christian faith learned about Jesus with their brains, working through what they were told and what they read through sensory perception. In the present day however, we have no experience with sensory perception that relates to resurrection. So, we are faced with accepting Jesus' resurrection on faith.

There are people with faith. The faith must come from somewhere. We can safely rule out that faith comes from one's ankle or liver. By default, if you have it, it comes from your brain. It may not be logical, but that's where it is. So, you have to reconcile it with what you perceive in everyday life. You also need to be aware that there are those who do not have it, and who are looking to take shots at yours. The defense that you have comes from the same brain that houses the illogical faith.

As with your muscles and your brain, it should seem that the same cliché applies to faith. Use it or lose it.

Reconciling faith with what science tells us

In some ways, it probably was easier to have faith in God before we knew that the world was round or that it revolves around the sun. Perhaps we didn't have to think about the possibility of life and indeed sentient life on other planets. To stretch it out, if we have our own prophets, who is to say that other planets with other "humanoid" life forms don't didn't or won't have their own?

Today, if we are going to accept faith in a supreme being, we have to try to reconcile that faith with our understanding of a vast universe that may or may not have originated with "The Big Bang" approximately 13.7 billion years ago. We have to think about the fact that at one time, dinosaurs walked on our planet. This clearly doesn't square with what we are told in the book of Genesis, but putting the Bible aside for the moment, we have to ask ourselves more importantly, how can we square this with our own heads?

I like to think of God as a gardener. Let's compare God deciding to create a universe to a gardener deciding to plant a seed. The gardener doesn't expect to have a seed one day, and a monstrous two hundred year old sequoia tree the next. The plant must first take root. Then the stem shoots out of the ground. Later, branches shoot from the stem, and the plant begins to leaf and flower. All along, it keeps growing larger and larger.

When God creates a universe with galaxies full of gasses and so forth, He doesn't expect sentient beings to pop up immediately, who can begin to contemplate his existence and understand the difference between right and wrong. All of this will happen in due time as part of the natural course of events, which includes planets cooling, atmospheres forming to the point where life can be supported, and on through the evolutionary progress of that life from one celled organisms through a period in which dinosaurs are stomping around, and on and on until humans or their sentient equivalent make the scene. And then, God only knows what comes next.

While I am on the subject, I must say I am curious about scientists who don't believe in a creative force. I have heard some of the discussion about the Big Bang Theory, the CERN super-collider in Switzerland, the Higgs-Boson Particle and so forth. It's truly fascinating, and I must confess that much of it goes right over my head. I don't have the scientific mind to grasp quantum physics and mechanics to any great depths. Still in all, I am reminded sometimes of the super smart kid at a magic show, watching the magician and finally blurting out, "I know how you did that!" If I was God, and I was doing the "magic," I would be sorely tempted to respond, "O.K., come on up here. Let's see you do it!"

What about when something terrible happens?

Humankind has somehow managed to survive all manner of self-inflicted atrocities as well as natural disasters to date. In every instance, whether it is one small child suffering from a debilitating illness that no physician can cure, 3,000 innocent civilians perishing at the hands of extremists who in their infinite wisdom decide to fly planes into skyscrapers, or 200,000 people perishing within hours of each other as the result of a tsunami wave, the same question always gets asked. How can a God, who loves us, allow this to happen?

It is altogether understandable that one would raise such a question, but if one believes in afterlife, they need to try to answer this question within the context of that belief. Assuming belief in an afterlife, and taking the moment in history when most people died at one time as the result of one event (the 200,000 lost in the tsunami) as our example, we have to accept that the souls of the people who were lost all ended up somewhere. Indeed, if whole families perished at once, then a case can be made that those whole families were reunited in eternity in an immediate fashion. Our sense of humaneness ought to be somewhat salved by that notion. The suffering for many of the people who passed away on that day may have been unimaginable, but for many others it may have been relatively quick and painless. We can't know for sure.

We are essentially "hard-coded" to avoid death. It is often understood that we fear death, but is the of fear death necessarily the same as avoiding it? When we attend funerals, we are told, and we try to believe that our loved one has gone on to a better place. Whether we believe that or not, we still must come to grips with our own grief at having lost them.

Many accounts of near-death experiences include encounters with friends and family members who have passed on before. If one believes in the afterlife, then it becomes illogical to mourn for anyone who we believe led a good life. It is altogether reasonable to grieve our own loss of that person, but as far as that person is concerned, we ought to be celebrating that they are in a better place in which we believe. If we further believe that most people are good deep down, then the notion of going to a better place after this life, must extend to most of the 200,000 people who were lost to this world in the tsunami.

It can be thought that death in and of itself does not serve any purpose of evil. Suffering and misery may serve purposes of evil, but not death. It has been for the remainder of the human family (the survivors) of the 200,000 to come to terms with the devastating loss. Evil may revel at the raising of the age-old question in the mind of the survivors, but if all of the 200,000 souls were good souls, evil could not celebrate those souls passing on to a better place.

What of afterlife, indeed

I read the book called, <u>Heaven is Real.</u> I am uncomfortable with it. At first it was coming across as inspiring to me. However, as I read on, the child's description of it felt too pat with the old descriptions that orthodoxy expects us to accept. It follows right along the path that would have us believe and accept the "my way or the highway" understanding of how heaven is supposed to be. There are and have been entirely too many souls on this earth who are and were raised outside of the Christian faith, who can infer from the book (and I expect the movie as well) that unless they convert before they die, the gates of heaven will be closed to them. If memory serves, Pope Francis, who heads up the Roman Catholic Church as of this writing, does not subscribe to this notion.

But for a more objective effort to report on what the afterlife might be like, I prefer to cite the documentary that Anderson Cooper put together for CNN. As with the story that is shared in <u>Heaven is Real</u>, the documentary shares near death experience with the audience. However, the documentary shares three such experiences, not one. Further, one of the experiences is shared by a woman who is of the Hindu faith. Due to the depth and speculation involved, the possibility of afterlife, and what it might be like have to be taken up as two separate subjects. The discussion of who can be included and who must be excluded also has to be taken up separately. Perhaps those who claim to have all of the answers will take this opportunity to stop reading, and trash this entire endeavor to all who come to them so hungrily, in search of rhetoric with which they can agree, rather than opening up their minds to speculation.

The time seems appropriate to quote one of my favorite bumper stickers . . . "A mind is like a parachute. It only functions when it is open."

What about the Bible?

I have already shared some thinking with respect to the book of Genesis, but there is surely more that can be said about the Bible. I am sure I have long since lost the fundamentalists in the audience, but for those who have chosen to read on, I will first cite my experience in attending the Alpha program. I would recommend the program to anyone, but I would not suggest that you just go in and guzzle down the Kool-Aid without bringing along some measure of the antidote.

If you attend the program, you will be exposed to a series of videos in which a gentleman named Nicky Gumble gives talks to an unquestioning audience. Perhaps not because they don't have questions, but to be sure, they are not given any opportunity to ask them. Nicky Gumble has many of his own thoughts about Christianity and the Bible just as I do, and I anticipate anyone who is reading this has as well. He does not suggest that the Bible should be accepted as literal truth. If I recall correctly, he confesses that there are contradictions within it. But he asserts that the Bible is "God Breathed". He goes into some discussion as to what he means by this, but again, the listener can decide for themselves.

Here's one layman's thinking on the subject. We know that much of the Old Testament was related orally from one generation to the next until someone decided to write it all down. Many genealogical lists and numbers of people within each clan or tribe are provided within the Old Testament. Reading them all makes one's eyes glaze over at first, before ultimately slamming shut. God's wrath not only to Jerusalem's enemies but also to the Israelites themselves is related over and over in the Old Testament, with harsh punishments being doled out time and time again.

Then, the New Testament is added on for Christians. To be sure, we do get doses of irrefutable commandments in the New Testament as well, from which we can glean that we are all going to hell in a bucket, since not only have we already sinned, but we are going to sin again, so what's the point? However, we also get the message that God is merciful. Depending on what church you attend, you may hear that as long as you are genuinely trying to be a good person, you can continually receive forgiveness for every time you inevitably screw up, so right there, there is some pretty obvious contradiction.

For those who are looking for specifics however, you can turn to Numbers 15:32, in which we are told that the penalty for gathering sticks on the Sabbath is to be stoned to death by your friends and neighbors.   At the risk of some regression, I'm pretty sure there is a cautionary tale here for those who would unconditionally trash the Koran, and have us all believe that we should not be concerned that any Orthodox Jew or Fundamentalist Christian would ever take extreme measures to ensure that the Bible is not violated in any way. In any event, there is no account of the teachings of Jesus anywhere in the New Testament that suggests that we should treat people in this manner.   If memory serves, I believe Jesus teaches us that if someone slaps us in the face, we should turn our other cheek. While this is a difficult standard to uphold, I think we can all agree that it is a far cry from stoning someone to death for gathering sticks on the Sabbath.

So, back to the notion of the Bible being "God Breathed". No matter what faith one takes up, those of faith often refer to themselves and each other as God's children. Although it is probably safe to surmise that God did not take up pen and paper and write the Bible for us, we can perhaps think of it as one of humanity's first and most important written efforts to decipher right from wrong. Further, some of the legend shared in it may be one person's (read unverifiable) recollection, however embellished and exaggerated, of events that actually may have taken place.

I have previously suggested that God may be more sophisticated than any (oh, so sorry) many of us. If we are not as sophisticated as God, and if we consider that we are God's children, then maybe we ought to consider the Bible as being a children's book. It is a source of stories, legends and poems, some of which contradict each other, but all of which in general, are intended to get us to think about how we ought to treat each other. To that extent, I can accept the notion of the Bible being "God Breathed".

A brief disclaimer

As I proceed with this effort, it has occurred to me that I am citing the quote attributed to Jesus in scripture about not judging others in one breath, and then turning around and sharing my thoughts about Fundamentalists and "Bible Thumpers" in the next. I anticipate that I am not finished sharing my thoughts about people who are not willing to consider new ideas. I may very well come up with even more colorful names for them as I go along. So, I must confess that I am not fully capable of living up to the very scripture to which I refer. Judging is judging after all, and although one of my editors pointed out to me upon reviewing my first draft, it is not possible to rationally consider something without making some sort of judgment; I do feel conflicted to some extent. Nevertheless, I hope that I will be forgiven in the end.

John 3:16; My way or the highway

John 3:16 reads, "For God so loved the world that he gave his only begotten son to the end that all who believeth in him shalt not perish but have everlasting life." To many Christians, this falls among the most comforting scripture in the Bible. It's fine as far as it goes, but to some, it would seem to suggest that "all who do not believeth in him shalt simply become worm food, probably over and over again."

For anyone who may decide to attend the Alpha program, you should know that at any one session, after you watch the video for that week, the facilitators split the attendees into small groups for breakout session in which they discuss the video that was shown that evening. Here's where it can really get interesting. Any Christian church is apparently welcome to host the Alpha program. This includes Roman Catholics, Eastern Orthodox, and in the instance in which I attended, The Church of the Living God.

At one breakout session, I asked one of the facilitators about people who have not become Christians. They pointed me to John 3:16. They happened to have a copy of the King James Bible on hand. For those not familiar, many copies of this particular bible have any quote directly attributed to Jesus printed in the color red. They affirmed for me that in fact, if you are not Christian; you are condemned to eternal damnation. Ohhhhh kaaaayyy!! I don't recall that I had any specific response prepared for the facilitator at that exact moment, but perhaps my facial expression or body language showed them that I was not satisfied with this assertion. I just have a difficult time imagining Jesus as a petulant child with his arms crossed in front of his chest first, and then pointing accusingly at some misbegotten soul and saying, "Daddehh!, he wouldn't accept me as his personal savior! I want him to go to hell!!!!"

At another time, I was visiting with the then pastor at Chrystal Lake Church in Ellington, CT named Joe DeLeo. I shared my discomfort with him about the notion that if one is not Christian, they don't make the cut. He said, "They get a second chance". Although I am not entirely comfortable with his assertion either, it is at least a step in the direction toward my way of thinking. According to him, when someone passes on who has not been Christian during their life, they do get an opportunity to acknowledge Jesus as God's anointed son. I don't know exactly how that happens.

I just hope that breaks are indeed afforded to anyone who was born into the "wrong" religion, whatever that might be. What about people who came before Jesus in human history and never had a chance to know of him? Do they all go to hell too? And how about people who are born so profoundly intellectually challenged that they never have the capacity to grasp the concept of God, or of Jesus and what he stood for? Hell for them too? What a nice and merciful religion we have here!

Here's one scenario for consideration that I would suggest to some of my more judgmental Christian friends. Say your name was Fred in mortal life. Then, suppose you die. Your soul ascends to the pearly gates. Upon your arrival, you are greeted by Jesus who reaches out to shake your hand. You think to yourself, "See, I knew it all along!" Then, over his shoulder, you see someone you don't recognize ambling up alongside Jesus. Jesus says "Say, Fred, I'd like to introduce you to an old friend of mine. Mohammed, say hello to Fred, here".

What are you going to do now?

Reconciling politics with spirituality

In May of 2014, Pope Francis released a letter to his bishops, called an encyclical, which has garnered a great deal of media attention. In it, he gave a great deal of attention to the concept of climate change (read global warming). It seems that he had somehow gotten the idea that God gave humans dominion over all things on earth, and that with that dominion, comes responsibility for the stewardship of the same.

In any event, some United States congressmen and presidential candidates when asked, essentially said that while they respected the pope, they felt that he should limit his comments to his area of expertise, that being spirituality.

Now it may be true that the pope is not an expert on climate change, but none of our esteemed politicians referenced any specific scientific studies that they had read, much less done any independent research on the matter so that we could count them as experts. The same goes for many of the pundits who chimed in in support of these same politicians.

Since very few of us actually delve into the science of this particular topic, the question becomes, what qualifies one to participate in the debate? The politicians may be concerned about the pontiff's celebrity. Many of us listen with rapt attention when a celebrity has an opinion on a political topic. This raises an interesting trivia question.

What do Hall of Fame wide receiver Steve Largent, Saturday Night Live writer and comedian Al Franken, body builder / actor Arnold Schwarzenegger and pro wrestler Jesse Ventura have in common? The answer of course is that they were all elected to high political office. Largent and Franken in particular, could be called upon to vote on legislation pertaining to efforts to regulate matters considered to impact climate change.

Pope Francis, by virtue of his position as leader of the Roman Catholic Church has celebrity. And like so many politicians, pundits, entertainers and professional athletes, he has (albeit thoughtfully and prayerfully) taken advantage of the fact that microphones and cameras are pushed in front of him.

Pope Francis is also a person. He had a childhood, went through adolescence, young adulthood, and ultimately ascended through the hierarchy of the Roman Catholic Church. He is a person who while clearly concerned with spiritual matters, also cares deeply about the people who live on this earth, as well as the other creatures that inhabit it, and indeed, the capacity of this planet to sustain life.

There is a song from the 1981 Police album Ghost in the Machine, in which Sting asserts that we are all spirits in the material world. This is a fascinating way to consider the human condition. As we grapple with the nature of our existence, we all also must deal with where and when we are living in a physical manner and how our behavior impacts those around us as well as our environment.

I would suggest that along with the rest of us, Pope Francis is entirely within his right to share how he feels about earthly matters. Despite the infinite wisdom of all our secular politicians, it would probably be best for their careers to not dismiss the opinions of people such as Pope Francis, even if their bailiwick is supposed to be "just spiritual".

Why are you worshipping?

Again on the theme of the possibility that God might be more "sophisticated" than any of us (assuming again that God exists), I have to take the blasphemous approach for a brief moment and wonder, If I were God, how might I feel about people worshipping me? Would I prefer them to worship me because they had to, or because they wanted to? Which is more genuine?

If you were sweet on someone, would you prefer that they reciprocate in kind, or would you rather apprehend them, lock them away and force your amorous activities upon them? Which would be more satisfying?

If you had a parent and they had to be put in a nursing home, how would you feel about visiting them? Would you only do it if the state militia came to your place of residence and escorted you at gunpoint to visit them or ought you to visit out of love, and respect, and as a gesture of gratitude?

I hope these rhetorical questions have made their intended point. If God is omnipotent as many believe, then wouldn't God know why you were showing up at church or synagogue or mosque?

Other people might think that you are holy, but remember that in the scripture, many of the clerics dabbed their jowls with talc in order to appear sallow and pious. Some people may have been fooled, but an omnipotent God would not have been.

For those who attend worship for what they think are the right reasons, this would be preaching to the choir. But there are also those who get caught up on the superstition that unfortunately shrouds orthodox religion all too often. "If I don't go to Mass this Sunday, I'll get a black mark on my soul". Seriously? Give me a break. Give God a break!

Go to worship because you believe it is the right thing to do. Go because it fulfills you in some way. Go because of the sense of community that you get from it. Go to get direction for your life. But don't go because God is taking attendance. This seems absurd to me.

Thanksgiving Day

For those from other nations who may read this, the U.S.A. celebrates Thanksgiving Day on the fourth Thursday of November. All banks, government offices, schools and stores are closed on Thanksgiving Day. Oops. Did I say stores? Silly me. Stores are now *open* on Thanksgiving Day. This is so all of us can spend time with our families and so we can step back and think about the things for which we are grateful. And then shop.

I understand that there is a ministry somewhere in New England whereby they make bag lunches which are as close to traditional Thanksgiving fare as they can get them to be, and then deliver them to people who have to work on Thanksgiving Day. This would include hospital staff, EMT personnel and the like. They typically deliver the meal with the message, "Having to work on Thanksgiving Day is a drag. Thank you for what you are doing.

But now, they can add people who work at Sears, K-Mart, Target, Wal-Mart, Macy's (who provides us with the wonderful parade down Broadway in New York City) etc. to their list. This is so that all the rest of us who have finished stuffing our faces and turned off the football game, which has gotten too lopsided to hold our attention can go out and start our Christmas shopping. We couldn't possibly wait until 6:00 on Friday morning.

There used to be Blue Laws all around the U.S.A. Stores couldn't open on Sunday. Then they could open, but they couldn't sell alcohol. One of the last ones to go was that the Baltimore Orioles and Baltimore Colts couldn't start their home games until 2:00pm if they played on Sunday. Most of these last were on the books because many of the powers that were, perceived the United States as a "Christian" nation.

I think that over time, the influence of non-Christians who either worshiped on Friday or Saturday or not at all, as well as the notion that another day of consumerism each week can't help but bolster the economy had the effect of pushing all of the Blue Laws off of the books.

No one can argue that having more time to buy and sell stuff greases the skids of the economy, and if that creates more jobs, then perhaps we need to accept it. Believers might still hope that somehow, some way, people are able to find one blessed hour a week to connect with their creator. This brings me back to Thanksgiving Day.

It is one day. One day a year. $1/365^{th}$ of a year. I just wonder. We have the internet now. We've actually had it longer than we've had retail stores open on Thanksgiving Day. If you absolutely must shop on Thanksgiving Day, could you at least do it online? If everyone stayed home from the stores on Thanksgiving Day, the stores would close. I know that some people would be out a day's pay, but in the end, everything that would have been sold on Thanksgiving Day, would still get sold sometime between Black Friday and Christmas Eve. Maybe the retail stores could give everyone a 0.3% raise to make up for the fact that they will still sell the exact same amount of stuff over the course of the whole year even though they are closed for that one day.

I would bet the ranch that if you took a survey, you would find that the vast majority of retail store employees who are called into work on Thanksgiving Day would much prefer to spend the day with their family. For the love of God, is it too much to ask to give our worship to the Almighty Dollar one day off?

Where do the critters go?

As I am writing, I have two companions who are dogs. By the time this gets to print, that may have changed. Growing up and at various times in my life, there have been dogs, a cat, and even a rabbit where I have lived. It is often a joy to have these creatures in your life, and it is agonizing when you must let them go.

This has made me think of the souls of animals. I understand there are many among us who do not believe that animals share in the afterlife with humans. This may even be written down somewhere in scripture or "sacred" text by (once again) a self-proclaimed expert on such matters.

It has been said that the eyes are the window to the soul. All of us have made eye contact with others of our own species. Each person can decide for themselves how they feel about the statement above. Beyond that however, I recommend to anyone who hasn't had the opportunity, that they visit a farm, a zoo, or an animal shelter. Attempt to make eye contact with some of the creatures that you see there. Think about how that experience makes you feel. Do you feel a connection? Do you get the sense that the creature is aware of its own existence? It is certainly aware of yours.

When I worked in the private sector, I had a friend who always liked to share stories about her pets with me. Once, we got onto the subject of the afterlife, and the question of whether there is such a thing or not. She said, "If there is a heaven, and they don't allow our pets in, then I don't want to go there when my time comes". I share her sentiment.

I had a dream once, in which I had the sense of being at a portal to the afterlife, about which I will go into more detail later. However, for now I will just share that there was a golden retriever that I have no recollection of ever meeting in this life, in that dream. I think we all should be open to the possibility that there is room for all good souls in God's kingdom after we depart from our mortal existence.

Beyond this, I would also suggest that the next time you have a steak or a hamburger for dinner, when you give thanks to God; also give thanks to the creature whose life was taken so that you could be fed.

Help America. Get up off your butt!

I recently saw a bumper sticker that said, "Help America. Pray the Rosary." I thought, "Seriously? That's how you're going to help America?"

I'm not saying that praying is a bad thing. A good way to pray might be to pray for strength to handle what life is throwing at you. Maybe praying for "serenity to accept the things you cannot change, courage to change the things you can, and the wisdom to know the difference". Maybe praying for forgiveness for all the times you have already screwed up as well as the times that you are still going to screw up. Maybe praying for the grace to forgive others whose screw-ups have caused you pain in some way. And sure, you can pray for America, although I doubt that America is the only place on earth with people who could benefit from God's grace.

But if you really want to help America, I suggest perhaps volunteering at the VA clinic or with the USO. If you have the means, maybe buy U.S. Savings Bonds. I'm just spit-balling here, but I think those types of acts would do at least as much for America as praying the Rosary.

A movie came out during the early '70's called "The Poseidon Adventure". It was an action adventure movie starring Gene Hackman, Shelly Winters and Earnest Borgnine among others. The movie was intense and took a PG rating. It would probably get PG13 today. But the reason I reference it now is that beyond all the action and adventure, the writers had a strong message to convey.

The story is of a luxury ocean liner at sea that is struck by a tsunami. Due to poor design, it is top-heavy, so it capsizes and remains upside down in the water. Then, it begins to sink.

Two priests figure prominently in the story. They both take leadership roles. One finds his way to the dining room and tells his followers to stay there with him and pray. He believes that they will all be saved by virtue of their praying.

The other (played by Hackman), leads a small group of people toward the bottom of the ship, which is the top, as it slowly sinks. He says that just praying by itself is not going to be enough to save people. Some of the people in the group perish as they help others (spoiler alert here) to finally get rescued from the hull of the ship by Coast Guard personnel at the end of the movie. However, all of the people who stay with the other priest at the bottom of the ship die as the ship floods and ultimately sinks to the ocean floor. You can draw your own conclusions.

Others are of course entitled to their own opinions. As for me, I don't think that God wants us to just sit around praying all day. God wants us to do his will and help other people when we get the opportunity. It's fine to pray, but we also need to do!

A brush with pre-destiny

Many people reject the notion of ESP out of hand. It is assumed that there are no such things as clairvoyance, synchronicity, or déjà vu. I don't claim to have any psychic abilities. Nor would I wish to have them. I will just share an experience of mine that should at the very least give you a sense of why I prefer to keep an open mind.

In the early '70's while I was attending public high school, my school hit on mid-winter vacation in February. I need to preface this story by telling you that on the day on which I am referencing, the weather was poor, with intervals of sleet and freezing rain. About the middle of that week, I was sitting around the house in the morning, probably a bit bored, when the phone rang. My best friend Dave was calling and said that our neighbor Tim had access to his father's car and wanted to go to see Dirty Harry starring Clint Eastwood at the Baldwin Place Mall, in Mahopac, NY. I'm a bit curious now to know if that mall still exists, but they had a single movie theater at the time, with the semblance of a malt shop adjacent to it. In any event, I was invited to go to the movie with, Dave, Tim, and I believe one other guy. Having nothing else to do, I accepted.

Shortly after that, I began to get a vivid and repeating sense of an impending car accident. No matter what I did, I couldn't shake the sense from my head. I managed to intermingle it somehow with what I would consider to be a typical adolescent fantasy, given that I had it pretty bad for Dave's sister at the time. My idea was that I would be there to comfort her in the event such an accident was to transpire. As fate would have it however, Carol either had a friend over or was at her friend's house and had no interest in going to see a Clint Eastwood movie with Dave, Tim, and me. Still, as the day continued to pass, this "premonition" continued to nag and nag at me.

I was beginning to freak out and wondered if I should tell the guys about it, but decided against it, figuring they would just think I was some kind of weirdo. I also rationalized that I was probably just bugging out over nothing. Still in all, when the time came to get in Tim's car and head over to the mall, I was not particularly comfortable. I kept my eye out the entire way over and was completely relieved when we entered the driveway to the very large and almost completely empty parking lot of the Baldwin Place Mall. I drew a heavy sigh of relief.

Then, Tim said, "Hey, Let's do some doughnuts!!" He accelerated and started into a turn.

That's when an old Buick with two elderly women in it came into my field of vision. I yelled, "Tim, watch out!" but it was too late. The two cars slid toward and finally collided with each other. The sleet in the parking lot reduced the traction considerably and served to minimize the damage to either vehicle. No one was hurt. I do recall Tim saying, "Hide the damn beer!!!" This was a curiosity as until then, I wasn't aware of the presence of any beer.

I guess the insurance covered everything, and the only further consequence that I was made aware of was that it was quite a bit of time until Tim got to drive his dad's car again, and that the beer which had been hidden under some bushes in a traffic island in the parking lot was never recovered.

It was a blessing that no one was injured. However, the incident stuck with me through the years and made the cut for this writing. Over time, I have come to understand it as a small demonstration for my benefit.

When people suggest that there is no such thing as pre-destiny or anything like that, I like to bring this little story to their attention. You can decide for yourself if you want to believe it, or exactly what it means, but I will just submit this as my own personal experience, which tells me that there are things that happen on this earth and I'm certain beyond it, that can't be explained by science.

What about violence?

This is a tough one, isn't it? With respect to taking a life we have some specific scripture to which we can refer, that being the Ten Commandments, which break it down succinctly, "Thou shalt do no murder". More with respect to violence in general, we have Jesus telling us in the New Testament to "turn the other cheek". Of course, neither reference is specific as to what will happen if we do murder or if we don't turn the other cheek.

With few exceptions, we always have some rationalization for committing violence. We also have our laws, which provide punishment for violence, as well as justification in certain instances, such as "self-defense". Then we also have international grievances which allow for killing the enemy who is after all, very evil. To be sure, everyone had their justification for killing German soldiers during World War II. They were after all, Nazis. However, it turns out that many of them were not Nazis or even soldiers as any result of their own choosing

There is a poem by a gentleman named Robert William Service called "Bonehead Bill" that tells us of "the bloke I shot last night".   In the poem, a soldier speaks to us in the first person. He has been fighting in a war. He knows that he has killed someone in battle. The next day, he is shot in battle by the enemy. He dies and goes to heaven. Who does he meet there? The bloke he shot the night before!

It is a curiosity isn't it? As I am writing, our president is dealing with the issue of ISIS. He has authorized air strikes in response to their actions. I am at a loss to even attempt to justify any of their atrocities. However, NPR joked recently during their quiz show named "Wait, wait don't tell me" that perhaps the president should turn his Nobel Peace Prize in his office around and have it face the wall so he doesn't have to be reminded that he won it. I must ask, we elected him to be president, not Nobel Peace Prize winner. What was he supposed to do when he was awarded the prize, say "no thank you?" In this mortal life, many times our elected officials don't find themselves in circumstances where they think they can just automatically do the peaceful thing.

On the other hand, we have had spiritual leaders who have been able to accomplish at least part of their political agendas over time through non-violent means. Dr. Martin Luther King Jr.

though sorely tested on numerous occasions, managed to never raise a hand to any of his tormenters. The Civil Rights Act was passed in 1964, largely due to his efforts, and although recent politics have served to compromise the voting right portion of that bill to some extent, we can generally still look back over the past 50 odd years and find evidence of success in the realm of social progress.

On a sports radio program (of all places) that aired shortly after the rioting in Baltimore, a commentator reminded the audience that if Dr. King had resorted to violence even just once, he would have been labeled a "thug", in all likelihood, the Civil Rights Act would either never have been passed or would have been delayed at least another 25 years, and, there would surely be no national holiday commemorating Dr. King's birthday.

For those who do try to rationalize and justify acts of violence I would just suggest the following . . . be prepared to approach judgment in a humble manner when and if the time comes. Your forgiveness may come more in the form of "Well, you thought you were doing the right thing" rather than, "you did the right thing".

The priest in the tornado

I have heard of one surgeon who works in a hospital and who is atheist. Part of his explanation for his absence of faith is that he claims that every time he sees a patient who is in critical condition or near death for any reason, they are afraid to die. This is an interesting observation, but perhaps not enough of one to not convince those who try to keep strong faith.

I recall some reporting by CNN several years ago about the brutal tornadoes that were ravaging the Midwest that season. They showed the extensive destruction in one town. Then they interviewed a gentleman who was a catholic priest. His rectory had been in the path of the tornado and had been destroyed along with the church. He however, had lived through the storm. He was rescued from the rubble by volunteers. As he explained it to CNN, he had done everything that one ought to do in an attempt to survive, heading to the downstairs in his home, and to the tub in the bathroom where he curled himself up as you are supposed to do: and then he began to pray.

Interestingly however, he did not pray to have his life spared. He prayed that God's will be done. If God meant for him to survive, he was praying for that, but if God meant for him to pass on, then he was accepting of that fate. This does not square with the contention of our friend, the atheist surgeon. Further, this may not be the only instance of someone who is able to balance the survival instinct that is hardcoded into each of us, with their faith in a supreme creator and an afterlife. I just felt that for the sake of discussion, one such instance should suffice.

How empty, or full is the glass?

As I was progressing with this project, it was suggested to me that I read the book called, <u>god is not great</u> (the g in God purposefully set in lower case) by Christopher Hitchens. I confess that I did not read it cover to cover, but I got the general gist of it. His thesis boiled down is that organized religion is responsible for all the ills of this life.

The author is an atheist. He points out all the misdeeds that have been done throughout the course of history in the name of God. He walks the reader through the Crusades, the Spanish Inquisition, etc. right on up to the misadventures of ISL in the present day.

It is clear enough that many have taken it upon themselves to take from others, right on up through killing others all in the name of God and the prophet whose flag they choose to fly. However, it can be argued that these atrocities could easily have been carried out without any religious affiliations based simply on economic grievances. The "religion" just provided a convenient righteous fervor upon which to fan the flames of violence.

However, to simply attribute all of life's ills to the twisting of religious dogma to serve one's own purposes seems an oversimplification. Also, while the author's argument is completely logical, it fails to provide any mention of the good that is done by many formally affiliated religious ministries. Many people have Catholic Relief Services to thank for the fact that they have food to eat and / or clothes on their backs. St. Jude's Hospital is an example of the good of everyday people allowing for health care for many who otherwise could not afford it. And the list goes on.

Later, I will discuss our capacity to look for the good in other people, but for the moment, perhaps we can consider the capacity to look for the good in organized religion. You can find it, if you look for it.

You never know

I remember seeing a segment once on a cable T.V. station (I believe CNN) in which the reporter was interviewing a former "skinhead". This was a young white male, covered with tattoos and shaved bald, with piercings all over his body, but according to him, no longer a skinhead. We can all make any of the stereotypes in our heads of this young person's behavior, but you need to keep in mind that for a relatively long time given his thus far short life, that behavior was driven by his own sense of stereotypes.

We go through our daily lives usually not giving much thought to how our behavior impacts other people, and the woman who he references in the interview may very well not be aware of the impact she had on him. As a skinhead, he had understood stereotypes about what different people are like, and what behaviors can be expected of them based on the color of their skin. This of course extended to people whose skin color happens to be black.

According to his account, he went into a fast food restaurant one day to order something to eat. The only person covering the register was a black woman, so he had to either deal with her or find somewhere else to order food. He decided to stay and order the food from the black woman.

Since the woman wasn't interviewed, we have no way of knowing what was going through her mind when he came up to the counter with his intimidating garb, and no doubt, his menacing persona. She could have felt an undercurrent of fear, although with the cameras that are in place in all these establishments now, she had that safety net to fall back on.

In any event, as the young man relates, this woman greeted him with every ounce of warmth that one can muster. She beamed a bright smile, and cheerfully took his order. When his order was up, she again happily handed him his food and wished him a nice day. The young man left shaking his head. He could not understand how this woman who was supposed to embody everything that he loathed in humanity could treat him with such kindness.

He pondered the encounter for some time, and in the end, the great wall of hatred that he had built around himself over time crumbled into a heap of rubble. His life turned around all because a woman at a fast food restaurant was nice to him one day.

You don't have to wave the flag of Christianity, or any other religion for that matter, right up in people's faces to have a positive impact on them. The way you behave on any given day, perhaps a day that has no significant importance to you could have a profound effect on someone else. Something to keep in mind.

Churches and money

We are always told by people of the cloth that churches aren't in it for the money. However, churches do need money in order to remain in operation. They don't have to pay taxes, but they do have to pay for everything else. Also, their personnel still pay taxes on their income, just like the rest of us. They get this money primarily from private donations and from fundraisers.

NPR reported recently that in order for an organization to qualify as a church, there are certain things it is supposed to do, such as provide educational services for the youth of the congregation (e.g. Sunday school) and to engage in community outreach. This can be in the form of soup kitchens, a quilting club, looking after shut-ins, or other such ministries. Another thing that ought not to be considered unreasonable for a church to do is to open its books to its members or prospective members upon request.

There are numerous churches, synagogues, and mosques throughout the United States that easily comply with all the above. Then there are other organizations. If you are a member and ask to see their books, they might say, "Well, we don't share that type of information because of this, that and the other thing". It all sounds very plausible, but hokum by any other name is still hokum. It turns out that there are other reasons to run religious outfits besides tending to the immortal souls of one's flock or to the social needs of the community. Lining one's own pockets with gold comes to mind.

Sadly, in many instances, we find that if an organization is using television or other major media outlets to get their "message" out, they fall into the category of organizations that are unwilling to share their financial data. I see this primarily in supposed "Christianity". For some reason, we don't see much in the way for televangelism on cable T.V. with Judaism, Islam or any other religion, but it stands to reason that corruption mushrooms up in those religions as well.

With respect to phony Christians, (they won't call themselves this) these outfits typically do not run education programs or local community outreach ministries. What they do is they put on a show. They don't bother with traditional sacraments, which take up precious prepaid T.V. time. They generally don't bother with the traditional garments of the clergy either. They wear expensive clothes that are somehow supposed to make them look more holy, shine bright lights, and have fully loaded orchestras and singing sections performing upbeat music which is anything but traditional, typically praising Jeehzuss and Gawdd from the top of their lungs. They spend an inordinate amount of time convincing you to make substantial donations to their "ministry". Many of them promise that God will make you rich. They often have "plants" in the audience who come up to the stage and miraculously get healed from some bogus ailment, and claim to become "saved" in the time it takes to flick on your living room lights, while the audience waves their arms all around in an ecstatic frenzy. How anyone can be fooled by all this mockery of true faith is appalling, but it goes on now, not only every Sunday, but really all week long, with 24-hour cable coverage.

In the New Testament, Jesus warns Christians to beware of "wolves in sheep's clothing". He says, "Many will come in my name . . ." The thing about it is that everyone, those on the up and up, and those who are in it for the money will say the same thing at this point. They will all say that they are looking to do good. It's up to the parishioner then, to take up their own due diligence. Again, we're back to using the brain God gave you.

If you think you know of an exception to the general rule with respect to televangelists, I would refer you back to my earlier suggestion, just as with any other outfit, that you ask to see their books. If they hand you their books and say, "Here you go, knock yourself out", a quick spot check will probably suffice to help you feel like you are in a good place. If on the other hand they start hemming and hawing and giving you a song and dance about why it is that they won't share their financial information with you, you may want to consider moving on.

The brown egg and the white egg

As I stated previously, it is fully my intent to avoid politics possible in this writing. If I do happen to tread on them however lightly, it should be on terms that I'm certain we can all agree upon, such as the right of every adult citizen to vote, and also on the subject of prejudice, which I am again *certain* that we can *all* agree is a *bad thing. . . .* Can't we?

To be sure, I think that if someone asked me today if I am prejudiced, I would say, "yes". Prejudice is something that many of us learned at an early age. We learned it from an older generation, many of whom didn't know any better. It sets us up for a knee-jerk reaction to anyone who looks different from us or who acts differently than we do. Now that we are adults; it is our task to recognize it within ourselves. If we can't or won't do that, then we can never overcome it. Hopefully, it fades away over time as we mature emotionally and socially. But you can't just turn it off like the flip of a switch. You must catch yourself in the act of applying it, and correct yourself each time, on the spot.

Without getting into the legacy of racism, or the institutionalization of it, I will just share this little story, which I first came across in the book, <u>Why are all the Black Kids Sitting Together in the Cafeteria? and other Discussions about Race</u> by Dr. Beverly Daniel Tatum, although I also heard a version of the story being shared with all of the children in my church by our Christian Education Director, before they were sent off to Sunday school one Sunday.

To the best of my recollection, the story (which I understand to be true) goes something like this . . . A young girl came home from school one day and shared with her mother that she had been having difficulties with a classmate. The difficulties were either centered on or tangential to the fact that she and this classmate were of different racial backgrounds.

The mother went to the refrigerator and retrieved one brown egg and one white egg from two different egg crates. She showed the eggs to her daughter and asked her what the difference was between the two eggs. The daughter immediately observed that one egg was brown and the other was white. The mother then cracked both eggs open in a skillet and tossed the shells into the trash. She showed the two cracked eggs in the skillet to her daughter and asked, "O.K., so tell me again which one is brown, and which one is white?" Of course, her daughter could no longer differentiate.

The lesson for all of us is that what is on the inside of each of us is essentially the same. We all have hopes, fears, and the need to be loved. Further however, for the purpose of this essay, I need to emphasize that no one has a choice at birth about the color of their skin. No one has a choice about their gender, their sexual orientation and any congenital defects such as physical or intellectual disability as well as genetic predisposition toward acquiring any specific disease. No one has a choice about who their parents will be. For many years, you have no choice about where you will live, and very few have a choice about where or how they may be educated. You also have little if any input with respect to whether you will attend worship services, and what sort of services they will be. It is all chosen for you. As such, anyone who judges anyone else based on any of these things is being patently unfair. This refers back to the suggestion that one judge not, lest they themselves be judged.

On greed

This is another one of those human flaws that falls in line with prejudice. It is a simple enough task to find greed in others . . . multi-national corporations, politicians, talent agents, and with apologies to my friends in the legal profession; lawyers quickly come to mind as well. But what about finding it in ourselves? As with prejudice, I am prepared to confess to being greedy. I would like to hit the lotto jackpot. Frankly, I would find it refreshing to hear a sermon from a rabbi or a priest in which they confess to the same.

Numerous Protestant denominations' common prayer reminds us to pray not for tasks equal to our capacity, but rather for capacity equal to our tasks. I do pray for that, sometimes. Other times I pray for my scratch ticket to hit it big.

Who wouldn't like to not have to deal with bills and creditors? Who wouldn't like to not have to get up at 5:00 am to go to work or open the shop? If you are raising your hand, jumping up and down and saying, "Me", hooray for you!!

There are a few exceptions to this. Mother Theresa was famous, but never rich. Bill Gates and

Warren Buffet have turned over sizeable portions of their fortunes to the public good, and are now being joined by a number of other billionaires who have signed on to the "giving pledge" created by Mr. Gates and Mr. Buffet in 2010. Pope Francis is known to drive himself around in a 1989 Renault. Dr. Martin Luther King could have lived pretty much anywhere he chose when he moved to Chicago. He chose to live in the ghetto. Those are ones of which I am aware, and I am sure there are others who manage to steer clear of the headlines. If I ever would hit the jackpot, I would hope that I would have it in me to give back, but I know I can't make that promise to myself or to anyone else today.

I just think, let's each go ahead and recognize the capacity for greed in ourselves, and then we have a chance to overcome it in the same way we have a chance to overcome prejudice or any other human foibles. Be honest with yourself. With very few if any exceptions, those who go around thinking or saying they aren't capable of greed or prejudice are among society's worst offenders.

On forgiveness

Forgiving someone is one of the most difficult things if not the most difficult thing we are called upon to do as human beings.

A couple of relatively easy things to forgive considering the vast array of atrocities of which our species is capable might be someone breaking off a relationship with you or unjustly firing you from your job. You may have heard it said or said yourself, "Well, I can forgive, but I can't forget". Or maybe, "It's up to God to judge . . . if that person ever wants to reconcile with God, perhaps God will let them off the hook". Either one of these statements is at least a start along the path toward forgiveness or reconciliation.

But consider the occurrence of a mentally ill man who several years ago, barged into an Amish schoolhouse in Pennsylvania, sprayed it with bullets from his semi-automatic weapon and killed a good number of young girls from that sect's limited population. Those who recall this incident probably also recall that those left to grieve also prayed for the soul of the deranged individual responsible for the act. *That's* forgiveness.

For those who may not recall that instance, forgiveness that parishioners shared following the more recent murders at the Episcopal Methodist church in Charleston, South Carolina during bible study, as well as the subsequent church burnings may provide a fresher reminder of the true meaning of the word.

This all falls right in line with Jesus saying, "Forgive them Father, they know not what they do."

I don't know if I could match what those people did in the way of forgiveness. I hope and pray that I am never put in the position to have to try. But at least I know where the bar has been set for me, and for all of humanity.

On confession and atonement

The Jews observe Yom Kippur every year. It is the most solemn day in the Jewish calendar. It is called a day of atonement. I don't know a great deal about the holiday beyond the fact that they aren't supposed to eat from sunset one day to sunset the next. Based on this alone, I am concerned that I would make a most irritable Jew.

I find the word "atonement" to be fascinating, however. I recall the poignant and powerful moment in the movie Godfather III, when Michael goes to the priest to confess that he had his brother Fredo killed. The weakness of Michael's confession is immediately apparent. He is able to go to the priest and confess to what he did. But he can't admit it to his sister Connie, the one who was must hurt by Fredo's death.

This is exactly what the Jews are referring to when they talk about atonement. If you know you have wronged someone, it's better to go to them and ask forgiveness than to take that guilt to your grave. We can and should confess our sins to God, but we ought not to forget about the other piece. It could be entirely understandable that someone might harbor ill will toward you about something that both they and you know isn't square between you. It might be worth taking the time to muster the courage, step forward, and come clean if that's what you need to do.

On ministry and charity

Ministry comes in all sorts of shapes and sizes. Sometimes it is institutional. Sometimes it is spontaneous or even perhaps (as in the case of the skinhead and the black woman) inadvertent. The old cliché that we always hear about is that of helping the old lady across the street.

By its definition, ministry is genuine. If someone is putting up a front, and passing some nefarious activity off as being ministry, then it simply is not ministry, and hopefully the truth of the matter can be ferreted out. But this article is about the genuine acts of ministry.

As indicated above, examples of ministry are innumerable, so if we have to consider just one genre, feeding the poor quickly comes to mind. Although St. Luke's Church in Somers, NY did not begin this ministry until well after I had gone on to college, I was made aware of a ministry that they had begun with their youth group called "Midnight Run". Father Hybel led the group down to the streets of Manhattan late on a Saturday night to hand sandwiches out to the indigent, and the homeless.

In the town in which I live as of this writing, there is a soup kitchen called Loaves and Fishes. I am not proud to say this, but suffice it to say, I have frequented them on numerous occasions. It truly is not my wish to pat myself on the back, and there is no genuine gain to me to do so, but for the sake of the message, I will share that I have taken their soiled rags and towels home for laundering.

People need these types of ministries have no desire to be in such need. Every circumstance is different, and the theme repeats again, that it is not for us to judge about how anyone came to be in such a state of need. It is very humbling to have to go to anyone with your hand out. But it doesn't have to be bereft of human dignity.

The time that you pull a sandwich out of your lunch bag and hand it over to someone who is out on the street holding up a sign they don't want to be holding, may be the time that they are so grateful, and that restores their faith in humanity. The kind word that you share may be what gives them the hope they need to go forward, and puts them back into position to catch the break that will never come their way if they just stay planted where they are.

I have passed on the opportunity to help people on occasion. I hope and believe that I have also redeemed myself to the point where I can put the guilt attached to those failures aside. We can't always be there for everyone, but when we are, it builds us back up toward being the kind of people we were meant to be. I hope that in writing this, I will have inspired some people, and re-inspired myself.

How do you know if you are doing God's will?

Most people would be concerned and put off if they were to come across someone who said, "God told me to do this" or "God told me to do that." I count myself among those who would be concerned. This is not to say that I haven't asked God what He wanted me to do.

It's safe to say that we were all born with an innate sense of right and wrong. If you are not certain about this, try this experiment. Find two dogs, perhaps from the same litter, or just two who stay in the same living arrangement. Have them both sit and stay. Then open a bag of doggie treats. Start giving the treats to one of the dogs, but don't give any to the other dog. Just have the one dog watch as you continue giving the treats to the other dog. It will not take very long until the behavior of the dog that is not getting the treats conveys its understanding of what is fair and what is not fair. If dogs can perceive what is fair and what is not, then it stands to reason that any human can do likewise.

We also learn from our experiences as we mature how ambiguities and shades of grey can come into play with respect to right and wrong. An outcome that turns out "right" for one person can be the same outcome that ends up shortchanging someone else, at least in their own perception. You can commit an act that seems innocent enough to you, but that ends up having a negative impact on someone else. Even a decision not to act can have unintended consequences.

But since we do have to act, if you are not sure about doing God's will, you can always refer back to the brief children's homily provided by Disney's Jiminy Cricket, "Always let your conscience be your guide." Then, even if someone does get the short end, you can at least know in your heart that you tried your best to do the right thing. At the end of the day, that will suffice for God.

On growing up

There are different ways that humans grow up. We are genetically guaranteed to grow physically, so long as we get sufficient nourishment. Other types of growing are not so automatic. We may or may not grow intellectually, socially or emotionally. We certainly may not grow spiritually. All these types of growth depend on our receipt of the "nourishment" associated with each. There is also the old saying that "You can lead a horse to water . . ." which applies in each instance. I refer to my previous citation of the quote, "There are none so blind as those who will not see".

But assuming one has and is willing to use the capacity to see, the nourishment to which I refer may come at different times and in different doses to each of us. Taking our friend the skinhead as an example, his opportunity to grow had to come coincidental to his willingness to do so. Perhaps he just had a good night sleep before his date with destiny. However it came about, he drank the water when it was offered.

One student who I tutored shared with me one morning that her friend had gotten suspended for fighting. We talked about non-violent conflict resolution, and at one point she said to me, "It's just my generation". I replied, "Yes, it is your generation, but believe me when I tell you that it was my generation before that, and my parents' generation, and on and on back through history". I also speculated that as much as Dr. King preached non-violence and acted in accordance with his beliefs, it is entirely possible that he got into a scrap or two on the playground when he was in grammar school. It's also a good bet that his old man gave him an earful when he found out about it, but that is after all, how we grow.

Social experiments have demonstrated in general how it is that children get to the point where they take an interest in what happens to and with their peers as opposed to being totally self-centered. For example, it happens sooner with girls than it does with boys. Clearly, it doesn't happen right out of the shoot. Sometimes, it never happens at all. A lot has to do with how we are raised, but sometimes, even with children of ill-prepared parents, it can still happen through the grace of God. Perhaps we should each leave ourselves open to opportunities to be agents of that grace.

A certain valedictory speech

I told this story to my 6th grade students that I tutor. I preface it by asking them to think of their best friend, and to try to think of anything that they would change about that person if they could. I didn't ask them for specifics, but to just tell me if they were able to think of anything. Most of them came up with something. They were able to find at least one fault, flaw, or foible. Then I told them about a certain valedictory speech.

As often as not, we had to discuss what a valedictorian is, and then I would explain that the valedictorian always gives a speech at their class's graduation ceremony. Here then is the story that I told my students . . .

My niece graduated from high school in the early '90s. Her graduation class was about 200 students. The valedictorian took the time in her speech to find something nice to say about each and every one of her classmates. She mentioned each one of them by name. Sometimes she grouped them based on some after school activity that they participated in together, so that her speech didn't take too long.

Now to be sure, she must have had her own group of friends within the class with whom she was most comfortable. There must have been some in the class for whom she did not have any great affection. There may have been a few who she had never gotten to know personally. But she still managed to find something nice to say about every single one of them. She did this by looking for the good in people. She was able to find it.

At the time that I listened to the speech, I found it to be a bit peculiar. But over time, I came to understand the importance of it.

We can find fault even in our best friends if we look for it. But we can also find the good in people if we look.

Oft times when we are driving on the road and someone in another vehicle makes what appears to be a mistake, we tend to take it personally. We find a colorful name to call them. Perhaps we lean on the horn and swear. Maybe we flip the "the bird" to let them know how stupid they are. But do we know them at all?

The "other vehicle" is a very impersonal thing. We don't even see the other driver's face until after the alleged offense has taken place. We don't know why they made the mistake or perhaps we contributed to the mishap and just don't want to admit it. All we know is what a stupid jerk the driver of the other vehicle is.

Next time you are in the heat of road rage, you might want to try to think of the story of the valedictory speech. The other driver is a person with a life, friends, family, etc..... There may even be something good about that person that you don't know. Perhaps this moment of reflection in the heat of battle will help prevent escalation of the situation. Keeping cooler heads and looking for the good in people are two things that are going to consistently point us collectively in the direction of peace.

The Nature of Faith

The question at hand is, "How do I know if I truly believe something?" With respect to faith, we must parse out information along the spectrum from fact to myth, with legend falling somewhere in the middle.

With respect to facts, there is no need for faith. We simply know that something happened. A third grader will tell you without hesitation that Columbus sailed the ocean blue in fourteen hundred ninety-two. This fact is supported by extensive documentation including primary source material. It is accepted as fact also, that George Washington was the first president of the United States. However, when be begin to consider the assertion that he chopped down a cherry tree and then confessed to his father stating that he could not tell a lie, the documentation becomes more questionable and we begin to move into the realm of legend.

Many of us have had the experience of believing in something mythical and having that belief shattered. The example that is most universal in Europe and the Western Hemisphere is the myth of Santa Claus. For many children, the experience begins with accepting the myth without question as presented by a trusted parent or grandparent. Typically, as they grow, they begin to be exposed to information that calls the acceptance of the myth into doubt. The myth breaks down for them gradually at first, and often with reluctance to accept reality, but finally collapses completely. Coming away from this experience, we are actually presented with an opportunity to understand how important it ought to be to subject other matters of potential faith to scrutiny.

Another scale that is useful to examining faith is the determination of what must be accepted as proof one way or another, as compared to what can be considered as evidence. For further example, while we are not presented with proof of intelligent design, we might examine nature both on our own planet and in the night sky (as previously discussed) and find what can be considered evidence of it. Then it becomes a matter of how each individual chooses to process that evidence.

Each of us is provided at birth with what I will call a nonsense detector. Some of us are unfortunately not encouraged or outright discouraged from engaging it. Sometimes the discouragement is cleverly disguised, and sometimes it even comes from those who are supposed to be our spiritual leaders.

Nevertheless, for those of us who have the capacity to employ our nonsense detectors, the trick is to dig down and examine whatever it is that we want to believe. If our beliefs can survive our scrutiny, or perhaps evolve in such a way that they can again become compatible with new information, we have a solid foundation for our faith. However, if we are not willing to make the effort to challenge our faith, we may end up abandoning it unnecessarily at a critical time.

How does love fit into all of this?

By extension, while atheists and believers argue with each other over the question of whether there is such a thing as a divine creator, we must also grapple over the question of whether love exists. There are some among the scientific community who tell us that for the purpose of procreation, everything is derived from sex drive, which results from hormones and biochemistry. So they will argue that it is not "love" we are dealing with, but rather just nature, and it's just that some of us who cannot understand all of this, mistake this drive that we have for something we call "love".

Excusing our scientific friends for the moment for their use of the word "purpose", which as previously discussed, hints at the notion of intelligent design, we are still left to ponder how it is that selfless acts take place. For instance, how do we reconcile how it is that someone would quietly or perhaps even anonymously donate to a soup kitchen when there is no discernable possibility that they will materially or sexually benefit from such an act?

I have done my best in this section to avoid the use of the word "why". However, many of us who might listen to music, read stories or poetry, or watch movies may point to the notion of love as an answer to the question of "why" someone would perform a selfless act. I'm sure that the scientists, who deny the existence of love, also avoid appreciation of music, prose, or art at every opportunity.

Although this article does not appear last sequentially in this work, it is the last article written from a chronological standpoint. I had thought I was finished with the work until I came upon the book "Born for Love", written by the late Leo Buscaglia. It occurred to me that one cannot write about faith and spirituality and not discuss the topic of love.

Mr. Buscaglia discussed love at length in his book, but never attempted to define it. Of love, it could be said that, "I may not be able to define it, but I know when I see it or when I feel it".

Love is not a fact. The Latin word "facere" means to do, while "factum" (the origin of the word "fact"), means done. Love is not done. It is in the act of being. It continues on. Since it is not a fact, it cannot be proven. In this way, it is similar to the existence of an intelligent creative force which also cannot be proven.

We are told by many theologians that "God is love". There is a simple beauty to the logic of this assertion. You can't prove God exists, and you can't prove love exists. All you can do is point to evidence.

Maybe however, this line of thought will help some who have historically thought of themselves as atheists to re-open the discussion. They can say, "I don't believe in God. I do believe in love". Then they can ask themselves the question, "Where does love come from?" Follow that question wherever it takes you. You just may find that you are not so much of an atheist as you once believed.

Faith and Spirituality on other worlds

For those who are willing to consider it, there is the matter of the possibility of sentient life on other planets. Usually, the notion of such a possibility becomes a separate conversation from the topic of faith and spirituality. But, for Gene Roddenberry and the writers of the various Star Trek series, the notion that such other planets with other sentient beings living upon them provided a rich opportunity to combine the two topics.

If we are going to allow for the possibility of sentient life existing on other planets, then we may also have to allow for the possibility that faith and spirituality are practiced there as well. They may have their own prophets and their own religions. Some of the more fundamentalist followers of our planet's major religions may find this notion particularly disturbing. One speculation that I have entertained is the possibility that Jesus has had to play out his part on other planets in addition to ours. Hopefully, he just has twins picking up that gig. I don't want to imagine him having to go through his ordeal more than once.

In any event, Roddenberry and the other Star Trek writers as well George Lucas and the writers of the Star Wars lore who lovingly provided us with the notion of "The Force" challenge us to give deeper thought to the nature of our God. The more people who are willing to follow these lines of thought, however briefly, the more people who become less willing to try to ram their own religion down other people's throats.

So, I just add this to the reasons why I try to turn people on to Star Trek and Star Wars. Please excuse my triviality.

The Hand of God

I need to provide some context for this discussion, and for this I am choosing to reference a book written by Mitch Albom and the movie that was made of the book called, The Five people you meet in heaven. The main character has passed on from this mortal life and is experience his first moments in the next. One of the people he meets is his former supervisor, or more appropriately, the crew chief to whom he reported in his work in an outdoor field such as construction or maintenance. When he meets his old boss, the man is wearing (as best as I can recall) a flannel shirt, blue jeans and work boots. They are outdoors, and the man is smoking a cigarette.

The man who has just passed on mentions the smoking to his old boss, and says something like, "I'm sorry you were not able to quit smoking". His boss tosses the lit cigarette to the ground, stomps it out with his boot, and says, "No one smokes here in heaven. That is just the way you remember me".

So, we each have our own way of remembering people. We may each also have our own way of "picturing" the Creator, again assuming one believes in the Creator. For me, being raised in a family that attended a stuffy old Episcopalian church, I would understand the Creator as being an elderly male with long white hair, a long white beard, and wearing a long white robe. Other people might picture the Creator differently, but for the purpose of sharing this personal experience, I would ask them to try to imagine God in this same way for the moment.

This book is not about me. I would be failing in my mission to share an extended autobiography. However, it is important (without going into great detail) for me to share here that I have been diagnosed with clinical depression. I manage my depression by staying active, making sure I get enough sleep and exercise, and taking a daily dose of fluoxetine HCL. As of this writing, I confess that my diet could still use some improvement.

At or about the time that I was diagnosed, I went through a time of what I would characterize as extreme personal duress. I have a sense that I had recently lost my very dear friend Archie, a black lab who had been my close companion for some thirteen years. Beyond that, it should suffice for me to say that it was my perception that everything that could go wrong in my life, was going wrong. And I had no answers. Or at least I thought I didn't.

God has never spoken to me or made a visual appearance to me. I know there are people who say that God has spoken to them. Some of them have related that God told them to start a ministry and to get people to give them lots of money to fund it. At some other point in this book I share some of my thoughts about televangelists, as well as my notion that God never tells anyone what to do. He might make suggestions, but he does not give orders.

This is my personal experience as best as I can recall it. I was distraught. I had come completely unglued and I was bawling my head off. I was having suicidal thoughts. But this time, for whatever reason, I did not blame God for my plight, as I am sure I had done on other occasions. This time, I simply cried, "God, I don't know what to do. I just don't know what to do." It was at this moment that I felt something. I felt it on my shoulder. It was only a feeling. It felt like a large, elderly, warm, masculine hand on my shoulder. It was there only for a moment or two, and then it was gone.

There was no voice telling me or even suggesting to me what I should do. It seemed to simply be conveying the message, "I am here, and I love you". It did not tell me specifically to apply for one job or another. It did not tell me to run out and buy a lottery ticket and use the following numbers . . . It made me stop what I was doing. It made me realize that I have the tools to decide what is best for me to do, and that I need to trust my own conscience. It made me tell myself to "just keep going" and to trust God. My problems were not all solved at that very moment. I just re-centered myself with the reminder that I have a purpose in this life.

Winston Churchill once said, "When you are going through hell, keep going". Many of us find ourselves going through what feels at any given moment, like hell. This happened to me, and sometimes, I can recall this moment when I need to. I hope that others will also benefit from my rendering of this story.

What is happening when we dream?

Scientists are happy to chime in on this question, but there is a human experience that is taking place that is outside of secular explanation. Examples can involve being able to fly or being able to cause objects to move simply by willing it to happen. One can find themselves on a skiing trail that stretches for hundreds of miles, on which they travel at blistering speeds, or perhaps a plaza where store fronts, kiosks and exhibits stretch out in every direction with no apparent end. When we dream, these scenarios become our realities. The world we live in when we are awake can be altogether forgotten.

Our bodies don't go anywhere during our dreams, but can the same be said for our souls? Oft times when we reflect on our dreams after we awaken, we observe that what we experienced goes beyond what we ever would or could have imagined during our daily lives.

We know that when we sleep, we turn over much of our decision-making capacity to our subconscious. The most obvious example of this is our breathing. It is possible to consciously hold our breath for a short time when we are awake.

However, when we are asleep, this cannot happen. It's the human body's equivalent of an airplane switching to autopilot. But circling back to the notion of our souls being photons (i.e. particles of light), perhaps our soul is wandering while our body rests. And the soul transmits its experience to our brains via a spiritual "tether" of sorts, causing REM sleep, changes in respiration and so forth.

It could be that the brain tugs on the tether and reels our soul back in in the event we are called upon to wake up. The tether is in place so long as our brain and body are functioning. When they cease to function (i.e. when we "die"), the tether is severed and the soul is free to roam wherever it chooses with no obligation to return.

This might seem far-fetched to some, but consider those most vivid dreams; the ones that end suddenly and which seem to cause us to wake up. If you've had one of these dreams, it may have ended with the sensation of falling or being suddenly dropped into your bed. It may be that your soul made the decision that the message of the dream is so important for us to retain, that it takes a sudden nose dive, back into our body so as to jolt us into waking up so that we remember the dream and think about it.

I can still visualize a dream I had quite a few years ago. I was in what appeared to be a barn loft. It was relatively new, and it had one of those translucent sky windows mounted into its roof. I was able to look down a ladder or perhaps a fold down ladder that might be built into an attic, down to a tavern room. The room had a bar on one side, and small tall round tables on the other side with stools set around them. The room appeared to be empty at the time. Sunshine was beaming cheerily through windows on the side where the tables stood. It seemed to be was morning, which may explain why no one was patronizing the tavern at that time. It may have been the 19th hole at a golf course with everyone still out on the course.

I had the sense that an invitation was being extended to me. I could climb down the ladder if I so chose, but there was a condition. The ladder was a portal. If I went through, I could not return. I thought of my friends and family. I thought of my dog, Archie. I was grateful for the offer, but my response was, "Now is not the time". Then I woke up. Upon reflection, it occurred to me that the offer, while genuine, was made with the foreknowledge that I would not accept it.

Perhaps our dreams are like windows into a realm of infinite possibilities, through which our souls can look while we are asleep. Perhaps reflecting on our dreams can give us greater perspective into this life and the next.

Does everything happen for a reason?

When considering this question, one of the first things a cynic might ask for is an explanation as to the reason for someone entering a school with a semi-automatic weapon and killing a bunch of people, or the reason that a group of people might fly two planes into the twin towers in New York City. These are fair questions. We must start with the understanding that humans are imbued with free will. The choices they make with that free will are not always good ones. Sometimes, mental illness is involved. Sometimes also, people voluntarily turn their free will over to a supposed leader whose intentions are questionable at best. And so, we end up with a lot of things happening for reasons that are difficult if not impossible to attribute to the wishes of a just and merciful God.

There can also be more personal instances that raise the question of the reason or reasons for something happening or not happening. Anyone who has ever been fired from a job, or passed over for a job or a promotion may well have had someone say to them that everything happens for a reason, and we may never find out what that reason is, so we are left to speculate. Was it because of a personal dislike? Nepotism? Age discrimination?

Was someone else genuinely better qualified? No matter what it was, it is a decent bet that someone's free will weighed into it.

One can fairly rationalize that it is not optimal to work for someone who doesn't like you, and the healthy attitude will always be that it is best to move on notwithstanding why things didn't go your way. Still in all, we all invariably think back on those moments at one time or another, and it can leave a bitter taste in one's mouth. Take for example, a teaching position. One might ask, "Was I passed over at the expense of the students?" And then you must guess at the reasons for what is taking place in your life now that you do not have that job. This can be an awfully tough nut to crack.

I will say here, that in one course that I took at a community college at the tail end of a medical coding training program, we were given the task of essentially tailoring our resumes and cover letters to a position for which we were applying, showing how any and all past experiences further qualified us for that position. The instructor was extremely persistent and would not let anyone off the hook. For some people it took some deep thinking, but come to find out, there are all sorts of life lessons that we can take from past experiences that can be applied to the new ones awaiting us.

To be sure, examples of things taking place that can leave believers scratching their heads are too numerous to recount here, but now I wish to now turn your attention, gentle reader, to an example of someone following a trail of spiritual "breadcrumbs" that may have been left for them and allow you to draw your own conclusions.

At a time when I was out of work and primarily looking for full time work, a friend of my eventually to be ex-wife noticed a marquee outside of a tiny Methodist church near where we used to live, advertising for a pianist / organist. She called to tell me about it and I eventually called. The gig involved travelling ½ hour each way to and from the church twice a week (once for choir rehearsal) and it paid minimally. . . I thought about it for a time and I could not say that I was thrilled about the opportunity, but I ultimately put in for it and was hired. Part of my thinking was that at least I could worship and make a little money at the same time.

I stayed on with that position for about two years. At one point during that stretch of time, I again found myself out of full-time work, and I was bemoaning my circumstances to a woman at the church who had befriended me. She suggested that I contact a friend of hers who was an elderly woman who needed help with chores and errands, in order to make a little extra money. Again, I was ambivalent. The woman was not the easiest person to get along with, but she did need the help, I needed the money, and it just felt like the right thing to do. I usually worked for her after worship on Sundays because she lived a reasonable distance from the church.

The route home from her house happened to take me past a Congregational church where coincidentally I had also worshipped for a time before moving away. After a couple of months, the Congregational church posted on *their* marquee, advertising the need for an organist. I pulled over, took down the number, and called them later that week. After I auditioned and interviewed with them, I was hired. The position paid more than the Methodist church paid, and they also had me playing every week, whereas the Methodist church was shorting me out of one or two services a month due to a guitarist who had dibs playing their once a month and also due to occasional children's services for which they used recorded music.

There is just a little bit more to this story. It is at the Congregational church that I met a very special friend, who is the woman whose assertion that everything happens for a reason, inspired this article.

Where is heaven?

You can find all sorts of discussion about where heaven is on the internet. In my research, I found quite a few videos in which people reference the Bible for their "answers" to the question of where heaven is. Then, I checked into the nature of space.

Space is often described as a place where there is virtually no matter. As such, it is considered a vacuum. No matter, no "things". Nothing. However, we do know that light travels through space. Is light a "thing"? It *is* energy. Energy is listed in the dictionary as a noun or a thing. Perhaps space can be thought of as a three-dimensional superhighway for light.

For example, the closest stars to the earth that we can see with the naked eye are Alpha Centauri A and Alpha Centauri B. They are approximately 4.4 light years away from us. So, if you find them in the night sky, you are actually seeing light that emanated from them just under four and a half years ago. Put another way, some of the light from those stars travelled through space in our direction for four and a half years, to the point where we could see it.

As previously discussed, Einstein determined that energy cannot be destroyed only transformed. We understand light to be a form of energy. When your mortal body ceases to function and the energy is released, could that energy be a form of light? Perhaps at our spiritual core, we are all photons (i.e., particles of light). Then the case can be made that once our energy is freed from our bodies, we as photons become free to travel through space. If that is so, then heaven can be pretty much anywhere we want it to be. Even in a supposed vacuum.

The "If it's meant to be it will happen" approach

Perhaps you have heard it said that "If it's meant to be it will happen" when you were applying to get into a school or for a job. A handful of times I found myself getting caught up in that Bachelor or Bachelorette show, wondering why one contestant or another didn't take that approach. Whether it's a matter of the heart or something else, one can to some extent, take the pressure off themselves by thinking that way. I have done it myself from time to time. There are, however, other considerations to keep in mind.

I am a bit of a sports history geek. There are several moments in sports history that never cease to fascinate me. For the purpose of this discussion, I will highlight two such moments. Both instances feature one team that was not considered to have any chance to be competitive, much less to emerge victorious.

On January 12th, 1969, the New York Jets played the Baltimore Colts, at the Orange Bowl in

Miami, FL in Super Bowl III. The backdrop is that the American Football League, from which the Jets had emerged had been in existence for nine years. By contrast, the National Football league had been around for 49 years. The AFL had started out as a rag-tag outfit that filled its rosters primarily with NFL cast-offs. Due to the deep pockets of its owners, the AFL was able to exert enough economic pressure on the NFL to force a future merger, and to send their champion the face the AFL champion at the end of each season, commencing two years prior.

However, public opinion still held that the NFL was vastly superior to the AFL. The Green Bay Packers had handily defeated the Kansas City Chiefs 35-10 in the first Super Bowl, and the Oakland Raiders 38-14 in the second. The Baltimore Colts finished the 1968 season with a 13-1 record, losing only to the Cleveland Browns, and later beating them 34-0 in the NFL Championship game.

Going into the game, public perception was such that Las Vegas oddsmakers had made the Colts 17 point favorites, meaning that they were expected to beat the Jets by more than two touchdowns. While it's well worth doing a deep dive into the specifics of the event, for the purpose of this article, I will simply share that the Jets won the game by the score of 16-7.

The other moment is the victory of the USA men's hockey team over the then Soviet Union's team in Lake Placid, NY during the 1980 Winter Olympics. Again, perspective is paramount. The Soviet team was a supposed collection of the best "amateur" players in the nation. Truth to tell, these "amateurs" came almost exclusively from the nation's perennial club league championship team known as the Central Red Army, with the balance of the players coming from the first runner up Moscow Dynamo team. These were seasoned veterans, the best of the best, who had played with or against each other for years and years. Going into the Olympics, they were thought to be "head and shoulders" above all competition.

By contrast, the US team, in order to meet the Olympic definition of "amateur" had to come from the ranks of recent college graduates who had never been paid to play hockey. There were no NHL veterans on the team. One player, the captain, Mike Eruzioni had played for the 1976 US amateur team in the World Championship tournament.

One last bit of information to provide context is that the Soviet team defeated the US team in an exhibition game at Madison Square Garden in New York two weeks before the Olympics started, by a score of 10-3.

It is well known that the USA beat the Soviets in the qualifier by a score of 4-3, on their way to the gold medal.

In both instances, there was at the very least, a perceived deficit in athletic ability that had to be overcome. And so, it is understandable to some extent, as to how some might conclude that the end result was "meant to be". However, both events also led many to sense that a triumph of the human spirit had taken place. And therein lies the nut that needs to be cracked.

If something literally happened because it was meant to be, we could assume that there was nothing that we needed to do in order to assure that it came about. It would just happen all by itself. But clearly, for the Jets to beat the Colts, different people had essential roles to play out. Joe Namath had to make his brash guarantee that the Jets would win, which boosted his team's confidence. Matt Snell had an integral contribution to make, as did George Sauer, Randy Beverly, and so many others.

The same goes for the USA men's Olympic hockey team. Herb Brooks molded and prepared the team for months and gave a fiery motivational speech before the game. Goaltender, Jim Craig, played the game of his life. Every single player on every line and defense pair skated like there was no tomorrow. If anyone had decided to go easy for one shift, it is entirely likely that the result would have been altogether different.

So, it might be O.K. to say that if something is meant to be it will happen, but only with the provision that those involved will heartily play their parts to assure the same. Vince Lombardi; the legendary head coach of the Green Bay Packers after whom the Super Bowl Trophy is named said, "Luck is what happens when preparation meets opportunity".

Huddle Up

In North America, and in the United States, we are conditioned to be goal oriented. You are always supposed to have a goal, and you always need to have a plan in place to achieve that goal. Without getting into specifics about what anyone's goal should be, I am always fascinated about the plans that get put in place, and how exact they are. Things don't always work out the way we plan.

In the book Jurassic Park by Michael Crichton, there is a mathematician named Dr. Ian Malcolm who explains "chaos theory" to another character named Dr. Ellie Sattler. He demonstrates the theory by placing a drop of water on her wrist, and by asking her to predict the direction in which the drop of water will travel. She tries to make a prediction, but the drop of water does not travel as planned. This is because of all sorts of variables for which she could not account. The less variables we account for, the less likely we are to achieve our goals.

Imagine you are standing at the base of a goalpost at one end of a football field, and I give you the task of heading on down and touching the goalpost at the other end of the field. On the surface, this seems like an easily achievable goal. Now suppose that I tell you that before you start off, you must put on a blindfold. You might now be inclined to tell me that achieving the goal will be all but impossible. If you could never take off the blindfold, you would be right. In all likelihood, as you attempted to reach the other goalpost, you would at some point stumble and fall, or barrel into a Gatorade bucket, a player's bench, a blocking sled, or a tackling dummy. However . . .

Let's add the condition that you could take the blindfold off whenever you stopped walking. So, for instance, you might walk nine or ten steps and then stop, take off the blindfold and check your bearings. You might notice that you have veered off slightly to the right or the left. Then you could adjust your direction slightly to correct for the veering off that took place, before putting your blindfold back on and proceeding another ten steps or so and repeating the process.

In a lot of ways, life is just like that. We have a goal in mind, and we blindly set off to accomplish it. We can accomplish that goal, but only if we stop, reflect, and observe the results of our efforts. Sometimes we start off with the best of intentions, but we get distracted, or something someone else does upsets us and we feel the need to take our frustrations out on them. We lose our way. If we keep barging ahead with our distractedness or our anger, we may never achieve our goal. Indeed, we may altogether forget what our original goal was.

Attending a worship service can be analogous to a football team huddling up before running a play. The goal is to score a touchdown. They huddle up and call a play. If all goes according to plan, they achieve their goal. But there are obstacles. The other team does something to prevent them from scoring that touchdown. Still, they may have made some progress. Perhaps they went from first and ten at their own 20-yard line to second and five at their 25. Now they need to huddle up and call another play.

In the same way, spiritual people who want to make the world a better place need to stop and reflect periodically on what their goal is, and what progress they have or have not made. They need to check their bearings, so that they are ready to try to progress again. It may be that they have made some mistakes. We can learn from our mistakes. The more often we can recognize mistakes when we have made them, the less likely we are to make them again going forward.

I believe that we get our moral compass from our creator. It is always there for us, but it will not help us unless we check it from time to time.

How do you know if you are "saved"?

A lot of people probably cringe when they see that word "saved" with the quotation marks surrounding it. The first thing that often comes to mind is "Born-again Christians." Televangelists have a textbook definition of a "Born-again Christian." These are people who have accepted Jesus as their personal savior, and who are therefore "saved." They will unabashedly tell you that only "Born-again Christians" go to heaven.

The televangelists often have formal proceedings during their programs during which, they invite people from the audience to step forward and publicly declare that they have accepted Jesus, and it is at that exact magical moment that they become "saved". Tragically, many of these people later take it upon themselves to barge into a church where many people have been worshiping for their entire lives, including perhaps having attended Sunday School as children, in order to show everyone there how they should be worshipping as opposed to how they have been worshipping. I have personally witnessed this, and while it is not for me to judge the true intention of the people who do this, I can share without hesitation that it does not tend to go over very well.

It also does not go well when a "Born-again Christian" tells someone who is Buddhist, Jewish, Hindu or some other religion that they aren't going to heaven because they aren't "saved." It's that kind of heavy-handed sanctimony that causes division and ill-will between people. The division seems to always occur when some people present themselves to others as "having all the answers". Paradoxically, it seems to be questions rather than answers that bring people together.

When we try to differentiate between faith and religion, we often find that religion is trying to force answers on us, when it is only by asking questions that we can hope to grow in faith. Atheists rightfully criticize the answers that orthodox religion is so quick to provide. When we widen our scope and look out into the universe with our questions, we do not get indelible answers. Perhaps we are not supposed to. Perhaps we are supposed to wonder.

Here is what I wonder. I wonder if every living creature on this planet at the end of their natural lives, severs the tether to their mortal bodies and is restored to their essential "photonic" identity. I wonder if they then find themselves at the portal to another realm. I wonder if when they are there, a being explains to them that within that realm, they will find love but not hate, and good but not evil, and that no being there ever harms another being. I wonder if they are asked if they regret every time that their actions during their mortal life caused harm to another being. I wonder if those who seek forgiveness for every time they have harmed another being are invited in. I wonder if the only ones who will not enter in are those who are unwilling to let go of all they hate they may have harbored in their hearts during their mortal lives. Finally, I wonder if those who are "saved" are simply those who have the capacity for the humility and the capacity for love.

I am curious to know what you wonder.

One day in New York

I am coming to the end of this project now, and I need to share how it is that I got mixed up with it in the first place. I need to answer the question, "What is it that qualifies me to do this as opposed to someone else?" After all, I don't have any special training. I haven't attended Divinity School or even very much Bible study. I think that ironically what qualifies me is the very fact that I haven't done any of these things. Clergy who want to know what their congregation is thinking can look at what I have written here to get a hint. As for everyone else, I think that what qualifies me is good old-fashioned initiative. Someone else could very well have done this. I did. Many "Americans" like to think that initiative is what "America" is all about.

There is one other incident however, that may have set me in the direction of doing this project, and it happened about thirty years ago. I worked in insurance for 27 years. I started off working for the Equitable Life Assurance Society of the United States on 6th Avenue and 52nd Street in New York City. I was relatively content in my first assignment, but after about a year, the "task force" that I was on got disbanded, and I got railroaded into the major medical claims department. I had to either accept the transfer or lose my job.

I need to preface the rest of this story briefly by telling you that at the time, I was commuting from Upper Westchester County to New York City via the Metro North Transit System each day.

There was a brief stretch of training, and then my training class hit the floor. Without going into extensive detail, the upshot is that I was having a very difficult time doing my job and dealing with my boss. It upset me to the point where I would have a knot in my stomach from when I would wake up on Monday morning until I left work on Friday evening. I was going through a box of Maalox every two weeks.

Finally, a day came when I decided I could no longer perform my job, and that the only option available to me was to retire at the ripe of age of 24. This took place in the winter I would guess, around February.

There were no "casual" days back then. It was all suit and tie if you were male. I had a trench coat that I was wearing into work each day. At about eleven o'clock, I reached for my trench coat, and left the office. I left my files strewn about my desk and made my way to Grand Central Terminal. It probably looked to any casual observer as if I had just headed off for an early lunch.

I was on time to catch the 11:48 am Harlem Line train back home. The big board listed it as departing from track 42. I boarded the train intent on essentially abandoning my job. However, the train didn't leave at 11:48. It didn't leave at 11:58 or 12:08 or 12:18 . . . (you get the picture). Finally, a conductor walked down the center aisle and announced to everyone that the train had been "annulled" and that the 12:48 train would be departing from track 116.

I was in no great hurry. After all, I was making a decision that was going to affect the rest of my life rather profoundly, and this was the last train I would ever have to take out of New York City. So, I made my way over and boarded the 12:48 train. However, the train didn't leave at 12:48. It didn't leave at 12:58 or 1:08 or 1:18. Finally, I just heaved a heavy sigh, got up and returned to work. I decided that I had inconvenienced enough people for one day.

When I got back to work, I hung my trench coat back up on its hook and went back to paying claims. A few minutes later, a woman who I knew only casually, and who I'm sure wouldn't have come over to my cube under any typical circumstances stopped by and asked me where I had been. I told her that I had temporarily retired. She told me that she had been worried about me and had moved some files around on my desk to make it look like I had been there.

I got back to performing my job, but the knot in my stomach was gone, and it stayed gone. I had an almost overwhelming sense of relief. I resolved to solve my problem another way. I realized that quitting my job was not a viable solution. Within a couple of weeks, I posted for another position (a lateral transfer) in the company. The transfer took place within a short stretch of time.

Now I don't claim to know what forces may have been at work on that day. All I can say is that I have my suspicions. You can draw your own conclusions.

One other point for me to emphasize now is that I was not attending church regularly at that time in my life, and it was to be many years before I would again do so. So, if there was any intervention taking place, it was not on behalf of a zealous card carrying "Born Again". It was on behalf of a "regular guy". So, we can ask now, "If there is such a thing as divine intervention, is it always something that we can pin right down, or is it something more elusive to our consciousness?" Also, "is it something that always involves the deeply religious, or might it affect someone who can be described as at best, on the periphery of organized religion?" Maybe it happens to Jews. Maybe it happens to Muslims. Maybe it happens to Hindus, or Buddhists, or (dare I say it?) even atheists? This all leads me to my last specific article.

Ever wonder?

To my mind, wondering is the only place that true faith can come from. It can't come from simply swallowing the party line, hook and sinker. Please understand I am not slamming organized religion in totality here: although there are certain sects, cults, extremists, call them what you will from whom we should all be looking to distance ourselves.

I would recommend the movie "The Life of Pi" to anyone who hasn't seen it, not so much for the whole story as for the insight of the young boy who decides, and tells his parents that he is a Christian, and he is a Jew, and he is a Muslim, and so on. There are many among each religious background, who would dismiss his multi-religion approach to spirituality. But it seems to me that he has his bases covered quite well.

Another movie worth checking out is St. Vincent. The main character (played by Bill Murray) has his flaws highlighted throughout the movie. He drinks too much, gambles, womanizes, and shows a rough exterior to the world. But at the end of the movie, he is put out to an audience at a private school by a boy he has met, as being a saint. He is for sure, not perfect. But the boy has done his own digging and has found the good side of this flawed man. He puts it up to the audience and shows them that there is good in this man. With very few exceptions, if you look for the good in a person, you can find it. Perhaps this flawed character named Vincent is destined to join all the rest of us wonderful people in heaven when he passes on.

I was raised Christian, and I can't claim to know much about the other religions. I am comfortable with the notion of Jesus as a savior who gave his life to save us sinners. It seems like a pretty good way to go. It works for me. I just don't buy the notion that it has to work for everybody. I don't accept that because someone isn't Christian, that they are going to hell when they die. I hope that I have given others reason to consider rejection of this notion as well.

I would say this, and I say this categorically . . . no one can tell you what to believe. You need to think about the world. You need to think about the universe. You need to think about the things that you have experienced that can't be explained by science. You need to think about love. Do you like music? Do you like art? Do you believe in love? If you do, then you must reject the idea that science can answer all questions. Science cannot explain music, art, or love. And it can't disprove the existence of a supreme being.

But there's more. You can't accept someone else's description of the afterlife or what is required of you in order to attain it. There are no true experts on this, often only self-proclaimed experts whose primary mission is to separate you from your worldly resources by duping you out of them. There are people who have studied and done extensive logical thinking for themselves, who can try to share some of it with their congregations. There are genuinely good people serving God within and without the context of organized religion.

You need to do your own digging. You need to ask to see the books. You need to ask the deep questions. You need to think it through for yourself. You need to test and challenge your own faith and accept challenges from others, over, and over, and over.

If you do all of this, you may find that you put others before yourself from time to time. You may find that you look for the good in people. You may find yourself becoming more generous with your time and your wealth than you were before. You may find that you have less "stuff", but you may also find that you are living a more fulfilling life. It will be O.K.

In closing

The pop singer Madonna tells us that we live in a material world. We do. We live in a world where if you don't eat, you die. If you can't pay your bills, no matter how you got to that point, society judges you as being unworthy of love. If you don't wear the right cloths, say the right things, have the right body type, you don't measure up. And if it was simply tough breaks that put you in the position you are in, then that is your problem.

But this is how society judges, not how God judges. Countless people go through their entire lives with no thought or understanding as to why they are here. It is possible to spend thousands of dollars in therapy trying to come to an answer for that very question. Or you can take numerous three credit courses at the undergraduate or graduate level grappling with the question. Philosophers have written paper after paper and book after book on the matter. You can study and search until your brain goes numb. Or you can ignore the question altogether and spend your entire life in pursuit of earthly riches. Then you can cash in at the end and take your entire stash with you on to the next life. Oops. That's not right.

For believers with genuine faith, it is really a simple question. You get up each day and pray for guidance to do God's will. No, God's booming voice doesn't descend upon you with clear direction. But you end up doing your given tasks, as mundane as they may be, to the best of your ability. Maybe you get a chance or two to show some kindness to a friend, or better yet, a total stranger. Maybe you get an idea about how you can gear your life in a direction to be an even more effective vessel of God's will down the road. Maybe you take another step toward the idea you already got a while back. It doesn't matter how much you get paid. It doesn't matter how harshly society judges you. All that matters is knowing that you are doing your best to make the world a better place.

In his poem, Oh Me, Oh Life, Walt Whitman offers us an opportunity to contribute a verse to the "powerful play" that goes on. He asks, "What will your verse be"? A believer doesn't care how great or small their part in the play is, only that they play it to the best of their ability. They can take comfort in the knowledge that it is on that and that alone,

that they will be judged. Go now and play your
part.

Acknowledgements

I would like to specifically thank Albert and Bonnie Haberle (my aunt and uncle), Pastor Kathy Faber and her husband Pastor Wayne Strever, and Susan Smith for taking hard looks at this work and sharing their critiques with me. .

I would like to also thank Susan Smith again as well as Jeff Dahlberg for their helping me with the self-publishing piece of this project with special thanks to Susan for her help with the cover.

Additionally, I wish to thank Margaret Murray for the use of her photograph of Mount Robson, north of Jasper, Alberta, Canada, which is used for the cover.

Finally, I need to mention that any sources that I have cited within the text served as inspiration for me in my efforts in some way, shape or form, including those of atheists and agnostics.

This work took about a year and a half from the initial brainstorming to the time of release via self-publication. However, the inspirations were gathered from a lifetime (to the present day) of experiences. The true list of people and institutions to which I owe a debt of gratitude is too long to list.

About the Author

Stephen Fowler grew up about an hour north of New York City and has always enjoyed writing, but this is his first effort at putting his ideas into a book. He worked for 27 years in the insurance business, primarily as an underwriter after earning his undergraduate degree. He is a talented pianist who enjoys skiing and playing chess.

He lives in the Northern CT vicinity. He currently works as a sales representative for a solar installation company while continuing to pursue a career in Education and an associated advanced degree.